"I've dated hundreds of frogs. And none of them was Mark Miller. He's not only a Prince—but a hilarious one at that. His book is a fun-filled bible of dating disasters, sure to make you laugh."
—*Marilyn Anderson, Dating, Flirting and Kissing Coach on TV's "Extreme Makeover" and author,* NEVER KISS A FROG: A Girl's Guide to Creatures from the Dating Swamp

"Any guy who's had 500 dates must know what he's talking about—or be in need of serious psychological care. Either way, you'll enjoy Mark's very funny and insightful book."
—*Robert S. Levinson, Bestselling author of* The Evil Deeds We Do, Finders, Keepers, Losers, Weepers

"I use humor to teach you how to speak successfully. Mark uses humor to teach you how to date successfully. Between the two of us, you can have a pretty humorous, romantic, outspoken life!"
—*Judy Carter, Motivational humorist, communications expert, bestselling author of* The Comedy Bible *and* The Message of You

"As a publicist, I've represented hundreds of major celebrities. Mark Miller has dated hundreds of women. Perhaps we should combine our talents and start a dating service for celebrities. Until then, enjoy his very funny book about the highs and lows of romance, specifically his, in the 21st century."
—*Michael Levine, Acclaimed Hollywood publicist, best-selling author, motivational speaker*

"Bravo, Mark Miller, for not giving up on love. 500 dates later and he still has the cock-eyed optimism of a hormone-infused teenager!"
—*Marla Martenson, Professional Matchmaker/Certified Life/Dating Coach, author of* Hearts on the Line

"Some guys are funny on stage, some are funny on the page. Mark Miller is that rare breed who's funny on both. Why he's not making out like a bandit on the dating scene is beyond me—but thank God he's not or we wouldn't have this very entertaining account of what's going on out there!"
—*Robert Masello, Author of* What Do Men Want From Women?, Robert's Rules of Writing, The Romanov Cross, *former columnist for* Glamour, Cosmopolitan, Elle

"I enjoy Mark Miller's stories about dating so much I hope he never finds love."
—*Sam Greenspan, Author of* 11 Points Guide to Hooking Up

"Mark Miller's anything-but-objective look at the dating scene is sweet, funny, and insightful."
—*David Misch, Screenwriter, teacher, and author of* Funny: The Book: Everything You Always Wanted to Know About Comedy

500 DATES

Dispatches from the Front Lines of the Online Dating Wars

by Mark Miller

Foreword by Julie Spira

Skyhorse Publishing

Skyhorse Publishing books may be purchased in bulk at special discounts for sales promotion, corporate gifts, fund-raising, or educational purposes. Special editions can also be created to specifications. For details, contact the Special Sales Department, Skyhorse Publishing, 307 West 36th Street, 11th Floor, New York, NY 10018 or info@skyhorsepublishing.com.

Skyhorse® and Skyhorse Publishing® are registered trademarks of Skyhorse Publishing, Inc.®, a Delaware corporation.

Visit our website at www.skyhorsepublishing.com.

10 9 8 7 6 5 4 3 2 1

Library of Congress Cataloging-in-Publication Data is available on file.

Cover design by Owen Corrigan

ISBN: 978-1-62914-466-5
Ebook ISBN 978-1-62914-848-9

Printed in the United States of America

DEDICATION

To my mother and stepfather, Diane and Edward, for being the best mother and stepfather on the planet. Yes, in fact, I did research all the others and, as suspected, confirmed their standing. And a special thanks to my mother, a former high school English teacher and college English professor, for instilling in me a love of reading, writing, and words.

To my father, Stewart, who departed the planet way too soon, but whose long-term, loving relationship with my mother showed me what a committed, romantic relationship could be—and inspired me to embark upon on a mere 500-date quest for it.

To my sister, Karen, the sweetest and most generous one in the family. Which I think is absolute proof she was adopted. But don't let her know; I'm waiting 'til the right time to break it to her.

To my son, Joseph, who makes me proud of him every day and is already way smarter than I'll ever be—a sure indication that genetic traits skip a generation.

To my daughter, Susie, who is so beautiful, both inside and out, that my friends and relatives demanded I take a paternity test.

To all my friends, ex-girlfriends, former dates, and ex-wife for making this book possible. Special gratitude and love for friendship and support above and beyond the call of duty to: Lauri Fraser, Barri Segal, Nira Be'er, Barbara Miller, Miriam

Gabay, Catherine Clinch, Richard Rossner, Rahla Kahn, Eileen Rosenbloom, Gail Langer Reznik, Melinda Benedek, Andrew Johnson, Terry Williams, Mel Sherer, Lyne Noella, Joan Becket, Leo Brereton, Andy Cowan, Rhonda Erlanger, Joan Reid, Marina Orebic, Katherine Lee, Steve Mittleman, M. K. Timme, and Melissa Wender.

To all the rest of my friends and relatives, too numerous to mention here, for their love, humor, encouragement, and support. Good friends are more valuable than gold. I tried explaining that to the folks at Visa, but they still insisted on their monthly payment.

Besides having that whole literary genius thing going on, another advantage William Shakespeare had was not having to deal with things like building websites, search engine optimization, and Google rankings to promote his writing. I therefore feel so fortunate to have made the acquaintance of Taylor Reaume, who is the Shakespeare of web strategy, social media and web marketing. In Shakespearean terms, he saved my ass. And I couldn't be more impressed with his work or recommend him more highly for those things for which most writers were not born capable. Connect with him at his company: www.thesearchenginepros.com.

Finally, to all you daters for, first of all, spending time with (and in some cases, money on) my book, and for having the courage and tenacity to put your heart out there to find its match. As I've found, it can be a long and rocky road, but the rewards are great.

ACKNOWLEDGEMENTS

Whatever this book is, it's way better than it would have been without the invaluable, insightful vision, suggestions, and input of my editor, Julie Ganz, of Skyhorse Publishing.

Kudos, as well, to my agent, Sharon Bowers, of Miller Bowers Griffin Literary Management, for recognizing the gem of something in my initial one-page idea summary, helping me grow it to an actual 38-page book proposal, and finding the perfect publisher for it.

Thanks to my friends, writer extraordinaire Patricia Danaher and her husband, attorney extraordinaire Bill Grantham, for providing the initial introduction to Sharon Bowers.

Gratitude to my friend, author Christiana Miller, for her generosity in sharing her knowledge of the book publishing and promotion worlds.

Thanks to my writers groups and organizations for the knowledge, support, and contacts they provide: Writers Guild of America, West; Writers Guild E-Pub Group; and Independent Writers of Southern California.

Gratitude to my writer friends who've taken the publishing plunge before me and generously shared their knowledge: Marilyn Anderson, W. Bruce Cameron, Judy Carter, David Castro, Dennis Danziger, Phil Goldberg, Lori Gottlieb, Annabelle Gurwitch, Jeff Kahn, Carlos Kotkin, Robert Masello, Christiana Miller, David Misch, Eileen Rosenbloom, Arlene

Schindler, Fred Stoller, and Steve Young.

To my celebrity friends and dating experts who were kind enough to provide cover blurbs: Louie Anderson, Marilyn Anderson, Dana Carvey, Lori Gottlieb, Sam Greenspan, Annabelle Gurwitch, Jay Leno, Michael Levine, Robert S. Levinson, Marla Martenson, Robert Masello, David Misch, Kevin Nealon, Kevin Pollak, Michael Richards, Yakov Smirnoff, Joel Stein, Fred Stoller, and Robin Williams.

Deep thanks to online dating and netiquette expert Julie Spira for writing the book's wonderful foreword that was better than I deserve (but I'll take it!).

A SINCERE NOTE TO ALL THOSE WHO WERE NOT MENTIONED IN THE DEDICATION AND ACKNOWLEDGEMENTS SECTIONS ABOVE BUT FELT THEY SHOULD HAVE BEEN:

Yes, I care about and appreciate you, too. But I'm only human and sometimes I forget. Hey, don't be like that. Where are you going? Come back! Okay, I'll add you back in to the next edition! I'm sorry!

And, finally, to Robin Williams, who provided a cover blurb for this book, showed all of us what limitless comedy could be, and departed this world way too soon. Though I was not comfortable using the blurb after his death, I did want to say a few words about him here. Robin and I knew each other from our early stand-up comedy and improv days in San Francisco. I have vivid memories of the first time I saw him perform. It was at the Intersection Coffee House, located in the basement of a church in North Beach, where there were seldom more than twelve people in the audience. All we aspiring comedians were absolutely blown away by the magnificence of the talent, imagination, and energy of this unknown person. It was crystal clear that he was destined for stardom. Other memories include attending his first wedding, cooking veggie curry for him in my apartment after giving him a ride back from a gig, going out for drinks with him and the other comedians after our club shows, allowing him to switch audition slot places with me on the roster at the Holy City Zoo comedy club so that he'd have a better time slot for the "Laugh-In" auditions. And then, of course, the many years of being entertained, overwhelmed, and touched by the scope of his talent. Most of all—besides the comedic genius part—Robin was a truly sweet, kind, and sensitive guy. It was a gift to know him and I'll miss him, both personally and professionally.

TABLE OF CONTENTS

DEDICATION   *v*
ACKNOWLEDGEMENTS   *vii*
FOREWORD By Julie Spira, Publisher and Editor-in-Chief at
   Cyber-Dating Expert   *xiii*
INTRODUCTION
From King of the Dweebs to King of the Dates   *1*

SECTION ONE: My 500 Dates   11
Part A: I Dip a Novice Toe into the Dating Pool   15
You Don't Have to Visit China to See Red Flags   17
Dating Women I Can't Afford   20
Does Dating Happiness Come From the Heart or the Wallet?   23
Love and Life on the Rebound   26
What's Love Got to Do with It?   30
The Hottest Date I've Ever Had   34
Making Scents of Being Single   38
A Challenge to My Fellow Dating Cowards   41

Part B: Look at Me—I'm a Dating Professional!   45
Stop Me Before I Share Again!   47
Dating? Think of It as Job Training   50
I Confess: I Love Jewish Women!   53
Unhappy New Year!   57
How Not to Rock Your Date's World   61
The Ghosts of Girlfriends Past   64
Speed Loving: Recipe for Disaster   67
Special Delivery   71
Don't You Feel Happy When Your Friend Finds True Love?   74
Do I Need a 12-Step Program for Serial Daters?   77

Part C: Help! I'm Drowning in the Dating Ocean!   81
I've Had 500 Dates—Kill Me Now   83
Coffee Date's Hidden Thoughts—Revealed!   88
Damn You, Foundation of Friendship!   92
I'm Not Asking for the Moon and the Stars   94
A Letter to My Future Soul Mate   97
A Personal Invitation to Share My Dating Pain   101
Help! My Girlfriend and Ex-Wife Are Hitting It Off!   105
Writing is My Lady   109
I Was a Woman's Last Online Dating Hope   113
Finding a Soul Mate is a Numbers Game, Actually   116
The Sounds of Dating Silence   119
Death of a Relationship   122
When the Music's Over   125
The Less I See You, The More I Love You   128

SECTION TWO: My Observations on Dating & Romance   131
Whatever Happened to Woo?   134
Mistakes Men Make in Romance   137
A Woman's Guide to the Inner Workings of a Man's Brain   140
How Internet Dating Beats the Pants Off Off-Line Dating!   143
It's a Woman's World—We Men Only Date in It   146
Thanksgivukkah: Not the Only Pairing That Can Benefit
You Romantically   150
Going for the Dating Gold   154
Male-to-Female Dating Dictionary   157
Never Underestimate the Importance of Proper Eye Contact   163
Saying it without Words   166
Oh, Come On, It'll Be Fun!   169
Official Soul Mate Determination Test for Women Only   174
Pillow Talk: A User's Guide   177
Relationships 101   181
Test-a-Jew   185
How to Seduce a Jewish Woman   189
Interpolitical Dating Tips   191
Psssst, Men—Beware of These Potential Dating Disasters   195

SECTION THREE: Dating Fantasies 199
I Finally Found the Perfect Woman 201
There Truly is Someone for Everyone 205
Just Another Fairly Tale Romance 208
The Continuing Adventures of Shlomo Rabinowitz:
    Jewish Private Eye & Dating Specialist 212
Dating Boot Camp 215
Skip Dating—Go Directly to Marriage 218

**SECTION FOUR: Fun "News" Stories I Wrote
About Romance, Dating, and the Sexes** 225
Female God Recalls Man for Repairs 228
5 Biggest Secrets Women Don't Want Men to Know 230
Amish Phone Sex Chat Line a Huge Hit 233
10 Best Opening Lines to Get Republican Women into Bed 235
Spain Claims It Originated French Kissing—and Sues France
    for $6 Billion! 238
Relatives Commit Woman for Dating Old Flame—
    an Actual Old Flame! 240
Police Arrest Woman Who Claims She Simply
    Loved Her Boyfriend to Pieces! 242
Couple Spontaneously Combust While Having Sex! 244
Men's Least Effective Pickup Lines 247
Woman Divorces Man After Discovering the "Mint"
    He Made Was Just Candy! 250

EPILOGUE 253
HOW TO KEEP IN TOUCH WITH ME 257

FOREWORD

Just how many dates does one need to go on these days before finding The One? More often than not, singles sign up for a dating site hoping they won't have a lifetime sentence. With more than 40 million singles dating online in the United States alone, dating has become more than a hobby to many. While it may be easy to fill your date card, finding your one in 40 million is a huge challenge for most.

Mark Miller has combined doses of humor with real-life situations to which singles of all ages can relate. Most single daters say they are looking for someone with a sense of humor as their number one trait. I'm here to tell you that Miller's stories are more than a hoot and a half. Most of these stories will make you roll on the floor laughing (ROTFL).

As an online dating expert who has written thousands of dating profiles over the last two decades and attended many weddings of online dating naysayers, I've seen more than my share of attempted misses at humor. Throughout *500 Dates: Dispatches From the Front Lines of the Online Dating Wars*, you will laugh with the author right into the arms of hopefully the perfect date, or at least be highly entertained by Miller's numerous, primarily unsuccessful efforts to do the same.

I first met Mark Miller at the West Hollywood Book Fair, where he attended my book signing. We immediately started trading dating stories and became fast friends. As a humorist, his essays in the *Los Angeles Times* made me laugh. His unique ability to find the perfect words to put a smile on a date's face was something I truly appreciated. Mark Miller quite simply is a funny guy. He's the guy you want to talk to about your bad dates or a recent breakup. He's the guy who always sees the glass as half full. Being able to laugh at yourself on a date that's gone south is a gift. Miller has been doing this his whole life. I promise you, this book will help guide you with the exact dose of humor needed to get back on the dating bandwagon if you've found yourself single again.

As mobile dating apps are now making it easier than ever to date on the fly and are reducing the geographic boundaries while looking for love, this book will help you shorten your search, spot the red flags in dating, and learn more about yourself in the process.

Before you head out to your next coffee date, read one of Miller's essays to lighten up the moment. Better yet, bring a copy of the book with you to share with your next online date.

—Julie Spira, Publisher and Editor-in-Chief at Cyber-Dating Expert and bestselling author, *The Perils of Cyber-Dating: Confessions of a Hopeful Romantic Looking for Love Online.*

Introduction:
From King of the Dweebs
to King of the Dates

The human transformation so vividly described in Robert Louis Stevenson's classic Victorian era novel *The Strange Case of Dr. Jekyll and Mr. Hyde* is nothing compared to the one undergone by myself in more contemporary times. Picture a nerd, a geek, a nebbish, a dweeb, a doofus, and a dolt—all rolled up in the same person. Now, flash forward to that same person having become one of the top dating and romance experts in America. Impossible, you say? And yet it happened! To me! Now do you believe in miracles?

How did a veritable virginal social and dating outcast become a nationally syndicated dating columnist for the Los Angeles Times Syndicate, *The Huffington Post*, and countless magazines, newspapers, and websites? How did my years as king of the geeks lead me to become one of the kings of the advisors to romance seekers and to performing stand-up comedy on national TV talk and variety shows, being hired as a writer-producer for a multitude of TV sitcom staffs, and as a creator of special comedy material for the likes of Roseanne Barr, Rodney Dangerfield, Joan Rivers, Jimmie Walker, Gallagher, Jay Leno, Garry Shandling, Jim Carrey, Dana Carvey, and many others?

One theory is that I was struck in the head by a meteor from the planet Lucky, which instantly transformed me into the idealized version of myself—better looking, more popular, smarter, funnier, more insightful, with the knowledge of not only how to become an expert dater and plumb the depths of the female mind, but also to impart that knowledge to others in a highly humorous fashion, or as the doubting voice in my head puts it, a "semihumorous fashion."

An alternate, more serious theory is that my emotional skin was toughened via my years and hard-won experience doing stand-up comedy and improvisational comedy along-side such comedians as Robin Williams, Roseanne Barr, Dana Carvey, Jim Carrey, Jay Leno, Howie Mandel, Sandra Bernhard, Arsenio Hall, and Jerry Seinfeld. Additional toughening was provided by a series of sitcom staff positions. These ranged from staff writer to story editor to executive script consultant to producer on such network and syndicated TV shows as: *The New Odd Couple, Diff'rent Strokes, She's the Sheriff, The Munsters Today, The Carol Burnett Show* (her later comeback attempt), *Living Dolls, Together We Stand, What a Dummy, The New Hollywood Squares*, and Dana Carvey's HBO Special. All of the above experiences served to put me to the comedic test of fire to the extent that it often felt literally like Funny or Die. I was relieved to discover that many considered me funny and therefore my life was spared.

Factor all of that into the subsequent 500+ dates and you get a lean, mean dating machine who has survived basically intact, with a sense of humor and some unique insights into what the modern-day dating man/woman wants and needs. Writing this book, then, has allowed me to take a breather from my formerly hectic dating schedule and look back over the past several years to put things in perspective, and offer my experience and insights to both men who may be going through the same thing and women who may be dating and/or curious about how the opposite sex thinks about and behaves in the dating game.

Among the true dating tales and revelations you will find in this book are:

- How my romantic partner informed me that I needed to share more of my emotional interior with her. But once I started doing so, I couldn't stop. She and I both learned the limitations of a man being too emotionally expressive.

- A woman I dated who'd been a wild, sexual temptress her entire dating life—until she met me, at which point she insisted on our establishing a foundation of friendship before we got naked for the first time. I realized to my horror that sometimes men have to pay the price for the behavior of their dates' previous relationship behavior.

- My attempt at proving my date wasn't a gold digger— by spending less than $20 on our date, purchasing everything for it at a 99 Cents Only Store, and what I learned as a result about the effects of a 99-cent box of 21 pieces of jumbo colored chalk on a potential soul mate.

- The intense pressure I experienced when, prior to our first meeting, my date informed me that I was her last online dating hope. Her entire romantic future was up to me and our first date. What does that do to a guy and how did I react to her?
- How a date treated me as her boy toy and how much I loved it—at first. How I experienced being in one of the traditional female roles, how I eventually found it hollow, and what that taught me about what I really wanted from a romantic relationship.

In the beginning . . .

Shortly after graduating from college, I found it rather strange and unsettling that despite having made my way through the world-famous U.S. education system, I was still completely unable to change a tire, balance a checkbook, or cook a meal. Oh, and one other thing on the surprisingly long list of important life skills for which school never prepares us—dating.

Sure, occasionally our parents, relatives, friends, or friends' parents would take pity on us and enlighten us in the ways of the world and the ways of the female, but you couldn't count on it. I certainly couldn't. For me, absorbing the wisdom of Dating 101 came down to trial and error—mostly error—which translated into frustration, awkwardness, embarrassment, anxiety, and failure. Hey, wait a minute—isn't romance supposed to be fun?

I was a naturally shy and insecure kid, made even more so by having to attend three different high schools due to my family's frequent moves for Dad's various jobs. Being skinny, having an iffy complexion, not excelling in sports, and not being a natural-born conversationalist (my father referred to me as "Marky Mumbles") didn't help.

And so females were a completely different species to me, a strange and unfathomable one. Dating was The Great Unknown. And the sum total of my sexual experience/training was my father having told me the facts of life on the way to going bowling together, followed by years of my sneaking peeks at the *Playboy* magazines he kept hidden under his bed. But even I realized that these were fantasy women. I knew I was never going to run into a stunning, smiling blonde with enormous breasts riding a bicycle naked in my town. And if I did, what would I say to her? "Hey, great bike! Care for some gum?"

Oh, sure, there were occasional bright spots. When I was sixteen, I looked out our house's window and noticed two pretty teenage girls in bikinis sunning themselves on blankets in their backyard. I recognized them from my school. Stealthily, I grabbed some binoculars and observed them like some stalker-in-training. How's that for creepy? But it was as close as I'd get in the tenth grade to seeing actual females my age in skimpy clothing.

During my junior year in high school, I asked a senior girl to the prom and she accepted! It was the high point of my life. We slow-danced and made out and drank Southern Comfort and apricot brandy. Forget my Bar Mitzvah—that night I was a man! I was making progress, I told myself, never anticipating the lengthy dry spells that were to follow me even through my college years.

Shortly after college, I accidentally fell into a serious addiction—to performing stand-up comedy. In retrospect, I highly recommend nightly stand-up comedy performances not only for developing one's sense of humor, but also for providing the antidote to terminal shyness and insecurity. The dating floodgates finally opened for me, and I took full advantage until something brought my playboy lifestyle to an end—marriage and children.

Let's flash forward through the marriage, divorce, solitude, and the end of the recommended "time alone to get to know and like yourself." Newly liking myself, it was time to re-enter that formerly frightening world of dating. Only now it wasn't quite so frightening. I had my humor, my confidence, and a committed, long-term relationship under my belt. All I needed were the women. There's always something.

Much like Columbus discovered the New World, I discovered online dating.

I'd like to pause now and take a moment to thank God for having created both women and online dating. Online dating—thousands of available women at my fingertips, looking for me! Or at least someone to date. I was not only like a kid in a candy store, I was like a kid in a dairy, a produce market, a seafood shop, a bakery, a Macy's, a Target, and a McDonalds drive-through. It was raining women, and who needed an umbrella?

Over the next 15 years, I experienced more than 500 dates. And, no, that's not a typo. Unless you're very lucky right from the start, you have to be willing to put in a lot of time, effort, money, and kiss a lot of frogs—or, if you're a male, frogettes. I suppose in retrospect, it was all book research. Which sounds a lot better than "an addiction to dating due to an inability to commit." And that's not the case, because, well, you remember that long marriage. I actually prefer being in a satisfying romantic relationship to dating. But in order to find that satisfying romantic relationship, you have to put up with the necessary evils of dating. But there I go quoting Aristotle again.

500 Dates is a selective tour via more than 55 humor essays of the highlights and lowlights of these 500+ dates. Yes, I sacrificed myself to endure several lifetimes of first-date jitters, pre- and post-date anguish, and crushing disappointment in search of the rare, elusive, hopefully not extinct soul mate.

You, of course, need not subject yourself to any of this personally. You are certainly welcome, if you wish with this book, to simply become armchair daters. After all, how many of you would truly choose, as I did, to become a woman's romantic fantasy plaything for one night, only to be cast aside forever by her immediately afterward? How many of you would decide to undergo a traumatic personal grooming experience simply to please a date? Or agree to a date consisting of together delivering groceries to homebound AIDS patients? Or take your date to a party at your ex-spouse's home only to find your date bonding and becoming friends with your ex-spouse?

But this about so much more than dating.
As its title suggests, however, *500 Dates* is not simply about dating, though that is its focus. It also covers romance, relationships, breakups, attraction, the nature of love, and how both men and women view the art, science, expectations, and reality of courtship and turning courtship into something deeper and longer lasting.

One thing I've tried to do throughout these essays is to provide a sense of optimism and hope about one's romantic prospects. Anyone who's done any dating for longer than a few months can understandably and easily fall into a pit of romantic despair, feeling that they're wasting their time, energy, and money, and that they'll never meet their soul mate, let alone someone with whom they're even interested in going on a second date. Romantic songs on the radio serve only to mock and depress them. Happy couples seen on greeting cards, TV, in movies and especially in real life only serve to twist the knife in deeper. Why do friends and relatives always ask, "So, how's your love life?"

Therefore, I've made every effort in my own dating life to apply my natural-born optimism, hopefulness, and gratitude to my romantic quest and ensure that those things inform my book's essays as well. Always, I ask myself, what is the lesson to be learned from this seemingly negative or uncomfortable dating situation? How can I spin it around to make something positive out of it? And I invariably succeed in making romantic lemonade out of lemons.

So, for example, if my date shows up looking substantially different from her profile's photo, I focus on getting to know her aside from that. I look for the good. If we have a nice rapport but after several dates no physical chemistry seems likely, I'll suggest a platonic friendship. Perhaps we can even end up helping each other professionally. That's happened on more than one occasion. If several weeks go by with no dating prospects, I'll focus on my work or hobbies or exercise or family. And if a date doesn't work out, I tell myself it's all right; I'm one date closer to one that will. I always head off to any coffee date with a smile on my face and a song in my heart. (And, no, the song is not "Love Stinks.")

But what do you get out of all this?
So, aside from that sense of optimism and gratitude, which I believe pay off big-time not only in the dating world but in all aspects of life, what do I hope you get from the humor essays in my book? Well, for one thing, I hope the book proves that

the end of a marriage, even a long-term one, does not mean the end of romance. Life is about second and even third chances, and success is often a function of how you process challenges and failure. If you're not failing from time to time, you're not trying hard enough to succeed.

More specifically, for everything we experience, we have choices for how we can react. If something frustrates or displeases us, we can and often do react with anger, tears, depression, or even violence. But those reactions invariably backfire, causing us to become even more physically and psychologically damaged, hurting ourselves and others. Instead, if we can start from a point of gratitude and appreciation for what we have and view any setbacks through perspective and humor, we do a greater service to ourselves and those around us.

I would hope that in reading this book, you recognize yourself and your experiences, or those of someone you know, in the universality of mine. Or even say to yourself, "At least I didn't have to endure that!"

How pleased I would be to know that reading my book cheered someone up, gave them some laughs, or motivated someone who had given up on dating or the hope of ever finding his or her soul mate. "If Mark could make it through 500 dates, maybe I could take a sip of his romantic lemonade and try just one more."

Then there's the technology issue. Face it, as time goes on, we're presented with increasingly more technology that allows us to avoid direct human connection. We can sit home with our iPhones and iPads and iPods and computers and Bluetooth 3-D digital TVs and Google Glass (Good Lord, a "wearable computer with a head-mounted display"!). And we never have to see, talk to, or touch another human being. That saddens me.

Because as nifty as all that technology can be, what is more important than direct, personal human connection—especially in the world of dating and romance? That's what I'd often say to a woman to whom I was attracted at a party. And she'd invariably reply, "I agree, and so does my husband who's approaching us with my drink right now."

And so while I don't pretend that *500 Dates* has all the answers or can guarantee that you will find romantic fulfillment, I think it's most certainly a step in the right direction for anyone choosing to experience the search for romance with enthusiasm, joy, humor, optimism and hope. Which is not to say that there won't be plenty of challenges along the way. And speaking of challenges, I'm pleased to inform you that I can now actually change a tire, balance a checkbook, and cook a meal. Still learning how to unclog a drain, though. Hey, come on—if I were perfect, you'd resent me!

—Mark Miller
Los Angeles, California

SECTION ONE:
MY 500 DATES

Warning: once you finish this section, you'll know me so well, you'll swear we grew up together—and ask me for the money I still owe you. Every essay in Section One deals with a date I experienced, loved, or endured, depending. Part A gathers together some of my early dates, while I still had on my dating training wheels. Part B explores my more experienced dating history, where I felt pretty confident about being a wonderful boyfriend, if I could just get beyond that first coffee date. And in Part C, I'm feeling as though I'm doomed to ride the dating merry-go-round alone for the remainder of my days. But don't cry for me, Argentina—or even New York, Atlanta, or Kalamazoo. Instead, come ride the dating rapids with me. I think you'll find it invigorating.

Part A: I Dip a Novice Toe into the Dating Pool

You Don't Have to Visit China to See Red Flags

Oh, sure, it started promisingly enough. Rhonda and I had each seen the other's photo and profile on a singles website, granted one another profile approval, and were now talking on the phone for the first time. Things were going pleasantly until Rhonda suggested that I choose a place for us to meet. I suggested a coffee house with outdoor tables at The Grove. She reacted unimpressed. I then mentioned a charming little place on Melrose, with a Japanese tea garden in the back. She yawned. Finally, I offered a quaint French café with outdoor porch seating and fabulous homemade desserts. The silence was deafening.

"Problem?" I inquired. "Those places just aren't very romantic," she informed me. Not very romantic? I was stunned. What are we, celebrating our anniversary? Getting together for Valentine's Day? It's our FIRST MEETING, for crying out loud!

We don't even know if we have ANY in-person chemistry! I told Rhonda that to me, any "romance" occurs as a function of the chemistry between the two people. And that chemistry happens (or not) whether the people are meeting at the Polo Lounge of the Beverly Hills Hotel, the Ritz in Paris, or at Taco Bell in Pacoima. She mumbled an unconvinced "I guess so," told me she was on her cell phone in the car, about to park in her garage, and would call me back as soon as she got in the house. I never heard back from her.

I briefly envisioned how I might have salvaged this particular relationship. A romantic gondola ride in the Venice canals with me feeding her grapes while comparing the texture of her skin to velvet? But if it turned out there was no chemistry, or very little chemistry, as is often the case, we'd merely be two people in a romantic setting, eager for the date to end. I just didn't get it. What was she thinking?

And then it occurred to me that this whole episode with Rhonda had been a gift to me from Cupid. You see, sometimes Cupid allows weeks, months, even years to go by before your romantic partner reveals his or her dark side. The longer it takes for the revelation, the harder and more painful are its effects on you when it all comes crashing down.

Other times, as with Rhonda, Cupid is kinder and allows the red flags to reveal themselves right from the start. So you're privy to your partner's deepest dysfunctions early on, in the harsh morning light of his or her true self. Any high-maintenance, humorless, judgmental, controlling, quick-tempered, dull, deceitful, insecure aspects of him or her rear their ugly heads. And at that point, you can decide if all of his or her other wonderful qualities make up for this—or if you would be far better off heading for the hills.

What fascinates me about all of this is that these red flags are revealed despite their owners' intentions of putting their best foot forward during those first few all-important, making-a-good-impression encounters. Sometimes, thankfully, their true colors can't help but slip through as merciful little advance relationship warnings ("The Crazies are coming! The Crazies are coming!"), thereby saving you all that time, money, effort, and emotional involvement (and subsequent hurt) for however long you might have become involved with them before the bad stuff surfaced.

Therefore, I thank you, Rhonda. You did me a favor, and I wish you nothing but the best. I sincerely hope you meet that guy who will be able to suggest a first-date locale sufficiently romantic for your deepest needs and desires. All I ask is that once you're seated with him at that charming seaside bistro on the French Riviera, with doves circling gently overhead and a strolling violinist playing "La Vie en Rose," you'll think of me kindly and wish me luck in my attempt to drum up a modicum of romance in some desolate Starbucks in Culver City.

Dating Women
I Can't Afford

Speaking of dates on the French Riviera, I encountered some women with such high financial expectations, that we may as well have been from different universes ...

One thing that's unique about dating as an adult, as opposed to dating back in high school or college, is that certain painful economic realities kick in. One in particular has caused problems recently for me—and that is the hard realization that there are certain women who, no matter how much we have in common, no matter how good our chemistry, no matter how right we seem for each other—are simply out of my economic league. In short, I can't afford them. And it's never me who makes that determination—they do.

When looking for a romantic relationship, I generally look for someone with similar values, interests, personality, temperament, sense of humor, background, etc. I generally don't check for a gold card when I'm searching for a soul mate. Yet it has become painfully clear to me that some people do.

Granted, this doesn't apply to all women. I've dated and had relationships with women who earned far more than I do, and it didn't matter to them—just as it never matters to me what a woman's income is. Still, it's a pail of cold water in the face when the cash factor destroys a promising potential relationship, as it did recently for me.

I arrived to meet Sandy at her house. Her big, expensive house. In a lovely, upscale neighborhood. Inside it was like an art museum.

Let me backtrack for a moment now. Normally, I might have been intimidated or had thoughts that a woman living in a house like this would never go for a lowly apartment-dwelling, Honda Accord-driving creature like myself. But I had screened her dating profile, drawing a blank at finding any of the telltale phrases women use to convey a lust for money: "high-maintenance" . . . "fine dining" . . . "frequent travel to exotic locales" . . . "enjoy being spoiled," etc. Sandy's profile seemed down to earth. And our phone and e-mail chemistry was great.

So, back to the house. I momentarily forgot about the surroundings because it soon became obvious that we had incredible, instantaneous chemistry. We were kissing within 20 minutes of my arrival. We held hands and walked arm in arm to get some brunch. And the talk was good, and telling.

Sandy told me about her wealthy ex-husband with whom she had very little romance. She described a succession of men she dated who had lots of money and took her to all kinds of fancy places, even to Europe. I started feeling a little uncomfortable, trying to imagine her reaction down the line when I suggested Santa Barbara as the exotic locale I could afford for a romantic getaway.

I was up-front with her, telling her that I couldn't provide that kind of lifestyle. I live simply. I go to inexpensive ethnic restaurants. I use grocery coupons. Sandy put me at ease. She said that those wealthy guys she dated didn't have a clue about relating to women. Most were overly consumed with their business dealings. She said she'd rather hang out in a small apartment with someone with whom she felt a genuine connection than be in Paris with someone not fully there for her.

As we walked back to her place, I remember thinking that there are certain times in life when everything seems perfect. And walking arm in arm with this beautiful woman who really seemed to "get it" as far as what was important, this was one of those times. The joy of that thought kept me floating on air for a full day—until Sandy called to let me know that, on second thought, our "lifestyle differences" were something she felt would keep us from being truly compatible.

In today's dating universe, the lack of cash can torpedo your chance for romance. But I'm sticking with the Beatles, as they sing in "Can't Buy Me Love." If I can find someone who adores me, that's as good as gold.

And yet, one day, I couldn't help trying a playful little financial dating experiment.

Does Dating Happiness Come From the Heart or the Wallet?

ating a woman in Los Angeles can be an expensive proposition. But must it be one? Don't all the greatest religious and spiritual masters tell us that true happiness comes from within? Does genuine dating success require that a man spend over a hundred dollars on his date? Is not a man more than a wallet and some testosterone? Do I ask too many questions?

I decided on a dating expense experiment never before attempted (or at least admitted) in the course of human dating history: I decided I was going to have a wonderful first date and spend less than twenty dollars doing so. That's right, less than twenty bucks on a date in Los Angeles. Okay, I know. I can hear women throughout the city exclaiming, "Cheapskate! Loser! No way!" Hey, they poked fun at Columbus, but he showed them. He found a way of impressing women without having to spend a fortune—simply by discovering a continent. Surely my date will admire my thriftiness, my resourcefulness, my imagination, and my creativity. I'll discover a continent of inexpensive fun.

And so, armed with twenty big ones in cold hard cash, I strode confidently and determinedly into the one place where I knew I'd get great value for my money—the 99 Cent Only Store at the corner of Fairfax and Sixth in Los Angeles, the store with not one, but two mottoes: "Shop Us First! The Smart Shoppers Do!" and "Nothing Over 99 Cents Ever!" I felt at home. I looked for the "Cheap Daters Welcome Here!" sign, but apparently it was being repaired.

Flash forward to the date. I arrive at Sarah's place wearing my playful Looney Tunes tie (a $9.99 value!), with a gift for her—an official Olympics Souvenir Program. A collector's item! It originally sold for $12.95, but I got it for, yes, 99 cents. Oh, sure, it was for the 1984 Olympics, but that makes it a 20th anniversary collector's item. Nor did I forget her cat, whom I surprise with a chicken and seafood Whiskas four-pack. Before we get in the car, I take out a big canister of 21 pieces of jumbo colored chalk, and right there on the sidewalk I create a multi-colored heart with Sarah + Mark inside. I bet her wealthy boyfriends never did that! So far, so good!

We drive to the beach (free scenery!), where the heat is no problem because I'm thoughtful enough to bring along Pinnacle Drinking Water, six for 99 cents, with sports cap. We sit there munching on Granny Goose's 13 oz. bag of tortilla chips and Sun-Maid six-pack of raisins. I even immortalize our fun with my new 35mm "Famous Name" 99-cent camera containing 99-cent color print film.

By my count, we had only gone through nine of my twenty dollars of purchases, when Sarah said, "Okay, what's going on?"

I said, "What do you mean?" all innocent-like. She mentions my tie, the chalk, the cat food, and goes in my bag and pulls out the remaining purchases, including Sesame Street Chocolate Chip Cookies, Krazy Glue, a solar-powered calculator, Famous Publishers Books, and Matchbox "Around the World" cars. "Are you losing it, Mark? What is all this?" I told her of my experiment and my plans later on for the Krazy Glue and the cars. And it's not that she told me that this was to be our first and last date, but I inferred it from the lack of response to my subsequent twelve phone calls.

I'm sure Sarah told all her friends. And they told their friends, and so on. Because whenever I'm out in public, I get the strangest looks from women. As though they're thinking, "So you're the loser who took Sarah on the 99 Cent Only Store date." I still believe that true happiness comes from within. But I realize now that on the journey of romance, thrift and creativity will take you only so far—for the rest of the trip, you'll need Visa and MasterCard.

Nevertheless, life has a way of balancing itself out. I may have disappointed Sarah, but in my very next relationship, we both disappointed each other. How's that for balance in romance . . . ?

Love and Life on
the Rebound

I was warned as a newly divorced man about the classic "rebound" relationship—one that shortly follows the ending of a previous one. Rebounders are supposedly needy, distressed, emotionally unavailable, and lacking the capacity to make good decisions about a partner. This not only describes me, but also most men I know in Los Angeles. Nothing personal, guys.

Still, I set out optimistically one night for a Jewish singles event called Opera under the Stars. Granted, I'm not a huge opera fan, nor am I a big stars nut, but it sounded classy and romantic and, okay, a friend talked me into going. The event's producer took over the backyard of a Brentwood home; brought in a tenor and a soprano to sing arias; served cheese, crackers, and wine at intermission; took our $30 admission charge; and wished us luck. Love for sale in L.A.

Luck appeared at intermission in the person of Amy, whom I immediately perceived as intelligent, attractive, funny, Jewish, available, and, most important, of course—interested in me.

The greatest benefit of an exciting new relationship? As any divorced man knows, going from a situation of infrequent sex and no sex—to one where you're suddenly with someone who actually wants to have frequent and enthusiastic sex with you. It's heaven, the life-saving oasis in your romance desert.

The abundant sex can also, of course, cloud one's vision, especially in conjunction with the aforementioned rebounder traits and the accompanying rose-colored glasses through which you're viewing your new object of desire. Those rose-hued glasses make it that much more challenging to make out the red flags directly in one's path. And so when Amy eventually suggested that I give up my writing aspirations and return to school to learn a trade, I said nothing.

Nor did I breathe a word of my disappointment one day when during our walk through an outdoor mall in Santa Monica, Amy looked around at our fellow mall-goers and disparagingly referred to them as "schleppers." *Schlepper* is a Yiddish term defined variously as an inept, stupid, ill-dressed, sloppy, and annoying person who always wants a bargain. It struck me as an incredibly rude, snobbish, and judgmental thing to say. But, again, I said nothing.

As the relationship developed, I kept my mouth shut about many of these kinds of things. Didn't want to rock the girlfriend boat. Preferred focusing on the things that were good, and there were good things, to be fair (Amy said to me on more than one occasion, "You're the man I've been searching for my whole life.")—that at the time I felt compensated for the insensitivities from "La Princesa," which is how Amy referred to herself.

My greatest regret about not speaking up was when my children invited me to join them at Passover seder at their mom's place. A little backstory: Although Amy was also divorced, she had no children. Didn't, in fact, seem all that taken with children and not especially eager to spend time with mine. Would even complain that on the nights I was having dinner with my children because she had to be eating all alone. By all this, did Amy expect me to not see my kids? Or to just have me feel guilty about her being alone?

In any case, Amy made it crystal clear that if I accepted that invitation rather than join her at her family's seder she would perceive it as a clear sign that I put her in second place—and our relationship would be over. I joined Amy at her family's seder, and to this day regret that decision.

Any man with just a bit of gumption and self-respect would have realized what was happening and walked away. But this is me we're talking about—the guy whose gumption was hidden behind his rebound relationship, his newfound sexual activity, and his rose-colored glasses.

The wake-up call I so desperately needed finally came— from, oddly enough, Amy herself, who did in fact walk away. I came home from work one day to find all her clothing removed from my closet. That was how she chose to tell me it was over. She was unreachable until four days later, when I got her on the phone. She'd decided to break things off due to my putting my kids over her and my refusal to give up the life of a writer and return to school to learn a trade. She said that each of her sisters were married to doctors and living in big houses in the Valley and she realized she'd never have that with me. And why she couldn't break up to my face? "It would have been too uncomfortable for me."

If it sounds like I'm bitter or resentful, far from it. In fact, I'm grateful to La Princesa for helping me get my head straight about my priorities in life and love. Billy Connolly once said, "I love Los Angeles. It reinvents itself every two days." I think we have to do that in life and in relationships, too, to stay on course. So, now I speak up a lot more. I have meals with my kids and am clear about them being my first priority always. And I wear those rose-colored glasses far less frequently. Oh, and I keep writing. That is, when I'm not hanging out with schleppers.

But I needed something to erase the pain of my failed relationship with Amy. The seemingly perfect solution soon appeared—a purely physical relationship.

What's Love Got to Do with It?

Women sometimes accuse men of being interested in only one thing. And it's not Scrabble. Okay, maybe for one man in Montana it is Scrabble, but Dwight's been married for forty-six years and, frankly, at this stage of his life, scoring a 27-point word gives him a lot more pleasure than scoring with his wife, Shirley. For the rest of us guys, though, I'll admit that occasionally we are only interested in one thing, and the one thing is sex. I'm sorry, but that's how we were constructed. Take it up with the manufacturer. Though I'm not sure we're still under warranty.

And yet I have encountered a live illustration of the flip side to this theory—a turnabout situation, if you will. I had a date with a woman, Laura, who made it clear on her online dating site profile from the start, that, like many guys, and unlike many women, she was not looking for her soul mate.

She was not looking for a long-term relationship. The word "commitment" was clearly not a part of her dating vocabulary. She merely wanted to, as that great philosopher Olivia Newton-John once put it, "get physical."

Perhaps there are lots of women like this out there, but it was certainly a rarity, if not a first, in my experience. A woman who just wants sex, no emotional or relationship strings attached. Now, most guys would describe this situation as, for want of a better word, heaven. And at first it was, well, kind of exciting.

Right from our first meeting, Laura made it clear that she liked me. Lots of touching, a hug, an invitation to her house for the second date. From there, she drove us to one of her favorite restaurants, chose the table close to the band, suggested sharing a bottle of wine, and shared her food. I was starting to feel like the woman in the relationship. And, frankly, it wasn't entirely unpleasant. We held hands during dinner, and she initiated the first and subsequent kisses during the meal. And though I was a full and willing participant, I was nonetheless taken aback. Throughout, I wondered on which cool planet I had landed where getting physical was so easy and stress-free.

On the way back to Laura's place afterwards, I thought to myself, *Rather than rush into anything, I'll act like a gentleman, thank her for a wonderful evening, and drive home.* Laura had something else in mind. She invited me in and asked me to light some candles while she went to the bathroom. I did and sat on her couch, thinking, *Okay, maybe we'll kiss a little, then I'll excuse myself like a gentleman and go home.* Well, that was the plan, anyway.

Laura came out of the bathroom, joined me on the couch, and, without saying a word, proceeded to have her way with me. Okay, yes, again I was a full and willing participant. And we did practice safe sex. And again, I'm wondering what cool planet this was where there was no need to discuss when we should have sex, why we should have sex, what sex means to us, what we mean to each other, and on and on and on. It was just raw animal passion. And I learned something. You know how they say that sex within the context of a committed relationship is even more wonderful? I learned that sex by itself is pretty darned wonderful, too.

But there was a feeling of emptiness in the aftermath: Laura did not invite me to stay overnight. She let me know that she couldn't see me 'til the following weekend because she was "busy" the coming weekend. And when I called her the next morning to thank her for what seemed to me to be a pretty exciting evening for both of us, Laura's exact response, and I quote, was, "Yeah, dinner was nice." And I thought to myself, *dinner was nice?* What is this, emotional payback for all the thousands of years men have been doing this sort of thing to women?

Two days later, Laura called and suggested getting together again. A more evolved man would have said, "No thanks. I'm looking for someone serious about a long-term relationship." But this is me we're talking about. We ended up going for cocktails and hors d'oeuvres and making out in the backseat of my car. There was no talk of a future date. I sent her a highly complimentary e-mail the next day. She never responded. And I still have not heard from her. But I thank her for teaching me something.

I learned about the feeling of hollowness and emotional whiplash one experiences going from full-contact lovemaking to no contact whatsoever. Don't get me wrong; I'm not saying I'd act differently if another Laura came along. But, truthfully, another Laura would not be my first choice. I like all that other "stuff" of a committed relationship. And I want it. Because as thrilling and comforting as sex can be, it is true what they say about having it with your special person—that is what your heart really needs.

Clearly, it was time for me to have a fully committed, emotionally involved, mature, evolved, deep relationship.

The Hottest Date I've Ever Had

The weekend had arrived, romance was in the air, and after a hard several days at work, I was so in the mood for love. I was looking good, feeling good, had a wallet filled with cash, and was ready, willing, and able to do anything my hot, beautiful date desired. Life was filled with sweet potential. There was just one tiny problem—I didn't have a hot, beautiful date. I didn't have a date, period. I was the sequel to *Sleepless in Seattle: Dateless in Los Angeles.*

While being dateless on the weekend is not an unusual state of affairs for a single person in a big city, I just didn't feel like surrendering to the standard carryout food and video option. I wanted to go out. I wanted to have some fun. And not with my male friends, commiserating about how hard it is to meet someone. Oh, sure, there were my platonic female friends, but I wanted romance. There were bars and parties and dances, but I'm not a bars and parties and dances kind of guy. There were escort services, but I wanted to be with someone who wanted to be with me, not some-one who was being paid to be with me. Unless, of course, it was Salma Hayek, but she has yet to respond to my offers of payment.

That's when the solution occurred to me. And it was one that, strangely enough, I'd never even considered before. It was this: I would ask out someone I knew would be available, knew everything about, was good-looking, healthy, had a won-derful personality, shared all my interests, was romantic and passionate, and was really fun to be with. That's right, my plan was to ask out the only one I knew who fit those qualifications and was available—I planned to ask *myself* out on a date.

I realize there are many of you out there who are already judging me. Maybe you're lucky enough to be married, in a committed relationship, dating. Or maybe you're even single, but saying to yourself, "I'd never stoop that low—to ask myself out on a date." Well, "judge not lest ye be judged." Walk a mile in my shoes. And, of course, it takes one to know one.

Oh, sure, I understood that there would be certain lim-itations, but any person you meet has certain limitations. I understood that some people wouldn't approve, but, hey, I'm not dating for their approval; I'm dating to make myself happy. Besides, think of all the money I'd be saving. And if it didn't work out, it was just one night, anyway. I could always dump myself. My mind was made up.

I spent the next several hours trying to figure out the exact words, the perfect way to ask myself out. It had to be just the right mixture of sincerity, confidence, attraction, and humor. After all, I didn't want to alienate myself right from the start. I wanted to set the right tone. So I prepared my approach, waited 'til just the right moment, when I knew I'd be in a good mood and receptive, and made my move.

I briefly considered using, "It's a felony in California to look that good, but if you go out with me, I'll let you off with a warning." I also flirted with, "I'm shipping out tomorrow to a combat zone; I could die." Or even, "Your eyes are the exact same color as my Rolls Royce." But none of them seemed right. So I finally decided to go with sincerity and decided on, "How'd you like to have the night of your life with someone who's been dying to be with you since the sixth grade?"

I asked myself out and, to my delight, accepted the invitation. I was dizzy with the evening's possibilities. My friend Ian called to see if I wanted to grab a burger and commiserate about how hard it is to meet someone, but I told him I already had a hot date for the night. He asked if it was a sure thing. I said I could pretty much count on it. Boy, was he envious! I shaved, showered, brushed my teeth, used mouthwash (twice!), and put on my best cologne and sexiest clothing that was soft to the touch. Oh, yeah, I was ready.

At my favorite Italian restaurant, I requested an out-of-the-way table so I'd have some privacy with myself. Things got off to an awkward start; after all, this was our first date. I referred to myself by another person's name. Awkward! But I managed to break the ice with a rather amusing story about losing my virginity during my break working at McDonald's, and before long, I was chattering away with myself as though we'd been friends for a lifetime. During the meal, my chemistry with myself was so strong that I scarcely noticed anyone else in the restaurant. We were in our own private world. I gave myself playful little touches and at one point, just before dessert, even played footsie with myself under the table, giggling like a schoolgirl.

The rest of the evening seemed to fly by. I found I had even more in common with myself than I'd imagined. We talked about our plans for the future, our hopes, our dreams, our fears. There was a real connection. Back home, I dimmed the lights; put on some smooth, romantic music; poured us both some wine; and lit a candle. No words were exchanged, no words were necessary, but we both realized what was about to happen, and we both wanted it. It was a magical, remarkable evening of love, and I learned that it is true what they say—sometimes you don't realize that your perfect romantic partner is right in front of your nose.

It's always very flattering to me when I hear something appreciative from my romantic partner the morning after a particularly wonderful evening of love. So I'd like to share with you the e-mail I received from myself the next day:

Mark, I just wanted you to know how very special and wonderful our time together last night was for me. As you know, as difficult as it is to meet someone you like well enough to ask out on a date, it's even more so to find a really deep romantic connection with someone. I felt we had that connection. Not to give you a swelled head, but I've never encountered someone who was so warm, giving, intelligent, interesting—in short, so amazing. It's no wonder our chemistry was so electric and the sex was so mind-blowing. If last night was a dream, I pray that I never wake up. All I know for sure is that I can't wait to be with you again, to experience the magic that we make together, to give myself to you totally, body, and soul. I want you. Passionately—Mark.

Of course, sometimes lacking a romantic partner (who isn't yourself) means that your other senses are heightened.

Making Scents of Being Single

hen a guy—let's say me, for the sake of argument—is lacking a romantic partner, every bit of attention I get from any woman, even a complete stranger, takes on heightened significance and pleasure. Because I don't have a wife, girlfriend, or lover, a simple smile from any woman passing me on the street is very likely to be the only, and certainly the most intimate, female contact I can expect all day. You might think that's sad. You might feel sorry for me. And yet I accept it. Hell, I more than accept it—I appreciate it, am grateful for it—okay, I even treasure it. Yes, that's right—I often treasure the smile of a woman I don't even know. Sometimes, if I'm lucky, she'll both smile and say "Hi," "Hello," or "Good morning." So I get to experience both her smile and her voice—double bonus. Triple bonus if you factor in the visual pleasures of seeing her. And a big quadruple bonus if all of the above is combined with what is perhaps my

favorite of the four elements—her fragrance as she passes by. That's right, the scent of a woman.

Okay, I know what you're thinking. *This guy's creepy. Some unsuspecting, innocent woman passing him on the street smiles, says good morning, and had the audacity to apply perfume, and suddenly he thinks he's in a relationship.* First, in my defense, I'm not quite that delusional. I realize I mean nothing to these women beyond being a friendly smiling face. And yet . . . sometimes, as that powerful quadruple bonus kicks in—the visual, the smile, the greeting, and the fragrance—I'll close my eyes, inhale that fragrance deeply as we pass one another on the sidewalk, and allow myself one quick and innocent indulgence—the momentary fantasy of what it might be like to be in a romantic relationship with this particular woman. And I would guess a lot of guys do this. Hey, come on, can you blame us? In ancient Egypt, women used perfumed creams and oils as a prelude to lovemaking. Am I expected to wipe that thought from my mind as a woman's lingering fragrance envelops me as she walks by? Of course not. In fact, if you were to order a transcript from my brain describing a few of these "encounters," you might find something of this nature . . .

Sally Citrus – A refreshing fragrance for an energetic, sporty woman. We bond over tennis, hiking, and biking. Over the years, we travel to exotic, little-known locations and thrill to new experiences. Eventually, we tire of one another and each drift into a series of meaningless affairs before bidding one another a deeply saddened farewell forever.

Leslie Lavender – A warm and caring scent of a woman who finds genuine fulfillment in giving to others. Together, we offer our free time to a multitude of charitable organizations, and then come home and offer ourselves freely to one another. Our relationship is founded on such honesty that even after she decides to return to her first husband, I share with her my progress on the antidepressant medication I take daily.

Olivia Oriental – A blend of excitement and mystery. Musks and precious woods are complemented by exotic essences. Our lives are luxurious, dramatic, sexy, and sensual. We live fast, eat well, and drive expensive sports cars. Unfortunately, one of these sports cars crashes suddenly while taking a mountain curve in Monaco, killing us instantly.

Have you picked up on the pattern? Each one of my romantic fantasies starts out with great promise and excitement, and ends disappointingly, if not tragically—just like my actual romantic relationships! What gives? Aren't fantasies supposed to be all good? Well, I can't worry about that right now. I'll let my shrink sort it out. And I especially don't want the women I encounter to worry about it. To them I'd just like to say it's not you; it's me. I'd also like to thank them. For their appearance, smile, greeting, and fragrance. And Sally, Leslie, Olivia—to the world you may be just one person, but to one person you may be the world. Even if it is just for thirty seconds. And even if you don't even know his name.

But passively inhaling a woman's scent as she passes is easy. It's a lot more challenging to take that first step and actually reach out to her. So, I decided to make that into a challenge.

A Challenge to My Fellow Dating Cowards

In Jerry Mayer's play "2 Across," a man and a woman who have nothing in common but their crossword puzzles are on a train leaving San Francisco Airport at 4:15 a.m. on its way to the East Bay. She takes crosswords (and life) very seriously; he treats everything like a game. By the time they reach East Bay eighty minutes later, their lives have changed. And it all starts with the man taking the first step of making a light comment to her.

It got me thinking about the times in my life when I failed, for various reasons, to take that first step of reaching out to someone I wanted to meet. Coming back from college one day, I struck up a conversation with an attractive woman my age at the bus station. We had a nice rapport, and when it came time to part, I couldn't bring myself to ask for her number. So our brief relationship ended there and of course I've never seen her again. This was back when I was still shy.

I've since gotten over my shyness. These days, I'm perfectly comfortable crossing the room to ask for a supermodel's phone number *while* she's chatting with Hugh Grant. After all, she can meet wealthy and famous movie stars any day. How refreshing would it be for her to hang out with a struggling writer? I'd even let her use my apartment's parking space and access to the building's washer and dryer. I'm a giver.

But say I *had* reached out to that woman at the bus station that day, asked for her number, and called her. There might have been one of many responses. She could have said thanks but I'm already in a relationship. She might have said thanks but I'm not interested. She might have offered her phone number but when I called it, I find I'm connected to her local police department. Are you sensing I have self-esteem issues? Of course, something positive might have resulted, as well. We could have gone out, hit it off, entered into a long-term relationship, gotten married, had kids, lived happily every after. Are you also sensing I'm a dreamer?

The point is, I'll never know what might have happened with that woman who could have turned out to be the love of my life—simply because I was too chicken to ask for her number. And when you think about it, my cowardice doesn't make sense, because in a situation like that, you have nothing to lose and everything to gain. It's all about taking that leap of faith and reaching out. Okay, so if you're rejected, perhaps your self-esteem takes a little hit. If you're rejected a lot, perhaps it gets bruised. And if you experience nothing but rejection, maybe your self-esteem ends up in the trauma ward of Love General Hospital. But enough about my pain.

Eventually someone is going to open her arms and her heart. Let's get back to that supermodel. How many times have we read interviews with supermodels, gorgeous actresses, and other high-profile beauties, in which they complain that they sit home alone because for whatever reasons—fear, intimidation, assuming women that lovely must already have boyfriends—they're just not asked out on dates?

Well, I say to my fellow male daters—let's end that fear here and now. Whether she's an average woman doing a crossword puzzle on a commuter train or Gisele Bundchen doing a *Sports Illustrated Swimsuit issue* shoot on a Jamaican beach—reach out. Put those insecurities on hold. A rabbi once said that "arranging marriages properly is as difficult as parting the Red Sea." Granted. But if you don't take that first step, the union is downright impossible.

But if you think making that first contact is a challenge, just try communicating deeply and sharing your innermost feelings while you're in a relationship. That's something I never realized I couldn't do—until one girlfriend after another clued me in.

Part B: Look at Me— I'm a Dating Professional!

Stop Me Before
I Share Again!

FTER the third girlfriend in a row gave me the identical critique of how I could improve my boyfriend skills, I decided that all three of these women were either:

A) meeting secretly with all my other former girlfriends to agree on which of my failings to rub in my face.

B) bringing up this same single trait that all guys lack just to have something to critique because, after all, if we were perfect, they'd resent us.

C) or, absolutely correct and I needed to work on my failing at once.

After immediately ruling out choice C and spending a few days stewing about choices A and B, I decided to show some backbone, suck it up, reconsider choice C, and do some work on myself.

Ann's critique originated during a session of the ever-popular (at least among women) relationship exercise called

"What Would You Change About Me?"—a cute little game designed by women to be absolutely impossible for men to win. Say the wrong thing and it's Game Over, Relationship Over, and you're back on Match.com for another six months.

All of which explains the carefully considered and worded selection of my critique for Ann: "You're so cute that it's difficult for me to focus on the meaning of what you say, 'cause I'm too preoccupied by your beauty, so I would make you just slightly less stunning." Seemed safe enough, no? No.

That seemingly inoffensive, innocent, and complimentary appraisal of Ann fed directly into her own critique of me—the same one I'd heard from the two previous girlfriends: "You don't reveal enough of yourself emotionally. You don't open up. I don't know who you are. You need to try to communicate on a deeper level."

Let me just state, first of all, that most guys consider revealing more about themselves emotionally and communicating on a deeper level nearly as enjoyable as falling face-first onto an ice pick—or spending the rest of eternity listening to Celine Dion music.

Still, I loved Ann, wanted the relationship to work, and realized that if I could please her by becoming the emotionally deep communicator she craved, it would pay off in the long run for me and for us as a couple.

That was all well and good, but when it came time to selecting the things to reveal, I drew a blank. I couldn't believe it. Was there nothing from my life or experiences or feelings or relationships I could share that would deepen my communication with her? Was I so on-the-surface? In terms of my inner life, is that all there is?

I dug deeper. I started small, revealing to Ann how as a child, I'd spend sleepless nights genuinely worried about death.

She responded, and shared things about her childhood. Which, in turn, sparked further revelations about my family, friends, upbringing, and our relationship. Over the next few weeks, Ann and I did more emotional sharing and deep communicating than a hundred meetings with Dr. Phil could elicit.

The more I opened up, the easier it got. And not just with Ann. I found myself sharing feelings with my other friends, family members, neighbors, co-workers, acquaintances . . . and the mailman, dry cleaner, masseuse, and even the cop who pulled me over for making a left turn from the wrong lane. Within three months, I had shared every conceivable insight, feeling, thought, and emotion.

One day, in the middle of a teary-eyed expression of regret over things I would have liked to have said to my father before he died, Ann surprised me:

"Stop," she said.

Excuse me?

"Stop. Just stop. I know I was the one who asked you to become more emotionally communicative, and you responded wonderfully to my request, but you went way farther with it than I expected or desired. It's too much. It's too frequent. And it's becoming annoying. I feel like I'm with one of my girlfriends. And I miss my boyfriend. I want the old you back. Please."

So I brought the old me back for Ann. She was happy again. And, in truth, so was I. It was kind of a relief, frankly. Oh, sure, there's something to be said for sharing. But there's also value in keeping your innermost feelings and memories private.

Maybe the key is finding the right balance. And not feeling superficial when your significant other asks what's on your mind and you answer, simply, "I could go for a good pizza."

I've learned so much from each woman I've dated. So many different skills. In a certain sense, dating's a lot like job training.

Dating? Think of It as Job Training

The life of the single person in Los Angeles isn't all nerve-wracking pain, disappointment, and heartache. OK, that's a lie. But there are a couple of positive things to be said about being single. For example, the world is filled with fascinating occupations, and I've gained invaluable experience in most of them, thanks to dating. My résumé is now 34 pages long. And that's just for the last two years.

Don't misunderstand—I'm not simply referring to what I've learned by hearing about my dates' jobs, though that also would be an important source of knowledge about a wide variety of occupations. I say "would be" because these women generally don't have my complete attention since, as they're speaking, I find myself pondering one of three things:

1. What's the quickest way I can end this date without her thinking I'm a jerk?

2. I wonder what she looks like naked.
3. Of all the Three Stooges, Shemp never really got the respect he so richly deserved.

No, I'm talking about the specific career skills I've learned, thanks to my extensive dating lifestyle. Take my recent relationship with Vanessa. Though far from being a professional actor, I nonetheless used my finest thespian skills to convince Vanessa that my favorite way to spend a Sunday afternoon was, same as hers, to take part in a public protest of some corporation's policy on animal testing. What a coincidence! My, we simply have so much in common! And you look so sexy holding that boycott sign!

Next, I summoned my best abilities as an amateur psychologist to make Vanessa understand that, owing to her never having received the love she so desperately desired from her father, she was determined to find a father figure in her romantic relationships. She wanted to understand more about her father fixation, but unfortunately I let her know that our hour was up and we'd continue it at the next session.

I'd always considered being a magician to be a glamorous career, and fortunately during my relationship with Vanessa, I gained loads of experience in making single-guy things disappear. Before her first visit to my place, I made all photos, letters, gifts, and traces of other relationships vanish into thin air. Clothes on the floor, gone. Dirt and dust, gone. Books, DVDs and magazines, the titles of which one generally doesn't find in family publications, gone. My ear hair, nose hair, and assorted hair from additional body locations—gone. Abracadabra! The Great Markini has done it again!

Thanks to Vanessa being high-maintenance, I had plenty of opportunities to exercise my skills as an accountant, estimating how much of my income I'd need to reserve for restaurants, gifts, trips, flowers, cultural events—you name it. And she did. I figured out how many deductions we could take if we were married, had kids, used a home office. I even envisioned a romantic ending: We'd both plead guilty for involvement in a fraudulent offshore tax shelter scheme, be sentenced to community service, and there, Vanessa would change into a caring, sensitive, low-maintenance person, telling me money doesn't matter. As you see, I lead a vivid fantasy life.

The point is that dating offers a lot of practical experience. The woman I end up with won't just get a man: She'll get a scientist, a security guard, a cook, a politician, a masseur, a mechanic, a social worker, and an athlete. Perhaps that's why it's taking me so long to find her—I want to make sure all those guys love her as much as I do.

Despite her occupation, though, I'll admit there is a specific kind of woman to whom I've become partial.

I Confess: I Love Jewish Women!

In my San Francisco days, I once had a brief romantic affair with a mime. I was living in a house with lots of bedrooms, which were rented out to many different people. One of them was her, Angie, a young woman who each day would leave the house, go down to the park, and do her mime thing, collecting dollars in a hat. I would tease her and we would flirt.

One day, coming out of the bathroom after a shower, I couldn't help notice Angie approaching me, taking hold of my bathrobe, leading me into her bedroom, and making her feelings for me crystal clear. A perceptive guy like myself notices these things. No words were exchanged. And I didn't feel awkward about the silent seduction, since she was, after all, a mime. We did everything that afternoon—walking against the wind, pulling a rope, being trapped in an imaginary box. I'd never enjoyed mime so much before or since.

If this sounds like some goyish fantasy, I agree. It does sound like one, but I swear it's true. Not that there aren't female Jewish mimes who seduce guys coming out of the shower, but I'm guessing it's not a large percentage of the female Judaic populace. Angie was Italian, and since that day I've dated both Jewish and non-Jewish women. None of the Jewish women came anywhere near being a mime. But they did offer qualities I've come to love and look for in my PRPs (potential romantic partners). Which is not to say that non-Jewish women wouldn't or couldn't have those qualities—but in my experience, these qualities are most likely to be found in members of the tribe.

Obviously, there's that unique connection to our shared culture, history, religion, traditions, and—my personal favorite— cuisine. Oh, sure, I could have taken Angie to temple with me, and she could have explained to everyone that just because she's Italian doesn't mean she knows cast members of *The Sopranos* personally and then entertained everyone with her impression of being trapped in an imaginary sukkah—but it's just not the same.

Jewish women, to me, always seem to have this inner glow, a warmth, a kindness, a sensitivity, an intelligence that I just don't find in their non-Jewish counterparts. And my Jewish radar, my Jadar, plugs right into it. I think Jewish women are prettier than others, and I love the fact that they're mostly brunettes. Blondes seem so, so . . . goyish. Finally, just try asking an Episcopalian for a plate of matzoh brei. She'll look at you like you're from another planet. "That's some sort of Jewish food, isn't it?" Yes, darling, but you don't have to be a rabbi to eat it.

My mother got remarried to an Irish Catholic man, whom I really like. She is very happy with him and even urged me not to limit myself to dating only Jewish women. How's that for turning the stereotypical Jewish mother on her head? Truth be told, I don't limit myself to dating Jewish women. Because, after all, variety is the spice of life, true love is rare, and you never do know where you'll find it. And while I'm not a betting man, if I had to place a bet on this, I'd say the odds are that I'll end up with a Jewish woman. And if she has an appreciation for mime, so much the better.

Of course, over the years, I've perfected my technique for wooing Jewish women. And because I am a giver, I will now share my technique with you:

"Oh, my synagogue sweetheart. The Jews may be God's chosen people, but you are my chosen woman. Our city's synagogue is the center of Jewish life, but you are the center of mine. Was it not the great Medieval Jewish scholar Maimonides who said, 'God will reward the good and punish the wicked'? We've been good; perhaps we can be each other's deliciously wicked reward from God.

And just as the choroset on the Passover seder plate represents the mortar used by Hebrew slaves, so the Barry White soul music playing gently in the background represents the feelings in my heart for you.

But my favorite Jewish holiday is Sukkoth, the harvest festival and time of thanksgiving. We thank God for all He has given us. It is then that I shall make a special thank-you to God for your presence in my life. For just as the rabbis teach us about Jewish laws and tradition, we shall instruct one another in the pleasures and glories of genuine Hebraic love. Judaism focuses on relationships: the relationship between God and mankind, between God and the Jewish nation, between the Jewish nation and the land of Israel, and between human beings. We continue that great Jewish tradition now, my little blintz, as we focus on the relationship between two

Hebraic souls who want each other more than a bagel wants a schmear of cream cheese.

We Jews believe that both man and woman were created in God's image—which explains how divine you are. According to traditional Judaism, women are endowed with a greater degree of "binah" (intuition, understanding, intelligence) than men. All I know is that I "binah" thinking about you all day long. Baby."

In fact, I love you so much, I'll even attend the opera with you. On second thought, maybe not.

But please understand, I don't just have relationship conflicts with women; I even have them with myself.

Unhappy New Year!

f all the days to pick a fight with myself, I had to choose the day of New Year's Eve, a time that should be spent in reflection and celebration. But no, my cantankerous spirit just wouldn't wait, and so, almost out of nowhere and with virtually no warning, I started in on myself.

"So, who's your lucky date for New Year's Eve?"

"Please. You know darn well I don't have any date tonight."

"What!? The Duke of Dating flying solo on New Year's? I'm stunned. How can it be?"

"I don't want to talk about it. It just worked out that way."

"It doesn't 'just work out that way.' YOU worked it out that way. How many dates have you had this past year?"

"Too painfully many to remember."

"And not one of them was available for New Year's Eve?"

"You don't just ask someone out on a date for New Year's Eve. It's a very meaningful night. A very expensive night. It's not for 'a' date; it's for 'the' date."

"So, with all those dates, how come none of them worked out into 'the' date?"

"You want a reason for each? She wasn't attracted to me. I wasn't attracted to her. She wanted someone who made more money. I wanted someone who talked about something other than herself. She wanted to have more kids. I wasn't communicative enough for her. She didn't have a sense of humor. I didn't have a passion for four cats. Shall I continue?"

"You know what you're doing, don't you?"

"What am I doing?"

"It's so obvious. For every woman you meet, you're finding some reason, any reason, to keep you from starting a relationship."

"That's ridiculous."

"Is it? You mean to tell me you meet a woman who's perfect in every way, except she has four cats, and THAT'S the deal-breaker?"

"Look, I never said she was perfect otherwise. And besides, if I didn't want a relationship, what am I doing spending all this time and energy meeting women?"

"You really want to know?"

"I asked, didn't I?"

"You're addicted to dating."

"Get out of here."

"Exactly. That's the message you're giving these poor women: 'Get out of here.' For you, it's all about the thrill of the chase. Ms. Right's just around the corner. The next one's going to be flawless. Well, get this, oh Sultan of Singles—there is no

Ms. Right, there is no flawless, and there is no satisfaction for you if you keep on this way. One day you're going to wake up to find yourself seventy-eight years old and on your way to your next coffee date. That what you want, Pops?"

"Of course not. But none of the ones I've met this year feel right. I've had dates where everything just clicks, we start dating, and before long, we're in a relationship."

"Sounds lovely. And where are those 'everything clicks' women now?"

"They didn't work out."

"They didn't work out? Or you subconsciously torpedoed the relationship so you could get back to your addiction?"

"I, uh . . ."

"'I, uh' is right. You know, I've about had it with you. You disgust me. Get out of my sight."

"I can't. I'm you and you're me."

"What did I do to deserve this?"

"Well, come on, don't give up on me. What do you suggest?"

"I don't know. Since I am you, I'm somewhat limited in my perceptions and insights."

"You don't have to insult me."

"I'm sorry. Okay, look, let's try something different this year."

"Why not? I've tried just about everything else. But no *Brokeback Mountain* stuff.

"I wasn't going there; that's your mind. I was simply going to suggest one small change in your approach."

"What's that?"

"One word: 'Stop.' Stop the dates. Stop the singles websites. Stop the matchmaking services. Stop the singles parties and dances. Just stop."

"Are you heading for a celibacy thing? Because that's not what . . . "

"I'm trying to keep you from a celibacy thing. Just live your life. Do your work. Be with your friends and family. Volunteer for something. Be out in the real world. She's out there, but you're trying too hard. Stop trying. Start living."

"I don't know. I'll think about it."

"That's all I ask. Now let's get some Thai food, and for the love of God, no Ryan Seacrest's Rockin Eve."

Maybe things would be better next New Year's Eve if I could somehow transform myself into the ultimate version of a dater—a dating rock star.

How Not to Rock Your Date's World

One thing I've learned as a graduate student at D.U. (Dating University) is that women respond really well to guys who have one or more of the following traits: a job, a car, a personality, a penis, a sense of humor, hair, a waistline, dancing ability, and fairly decent personal hygiene habits. Still, even having all of these traits is no guarantee the two of you will hit it off. If I wanted that kind of guarantee, I'd need to become a rock star—which would be extremely challenging since I can't sing, play a musical instrument, and am pretty much old enough to be the father of a rock star. No, I'd have to find some other way to inspire women to provide me with the level of passion and devotion shown by rock star groupies.

But a while back, I got to thinking, as I do approximately two or three times a year. And my thought was—*what if, as the* ancient wisdom puts it, instead of studying, training, or practicing to become a rock star, I would simply just be the rock star? After all, women do admire confidence. I could simply approach my dates with rock star chutzpah. And despite my voice, I could even sing to them, if I did it with enough confidence—the serenade being yet another tried and true, ancient romantic technique. After three such dates, I am filing the following report:

Date #1: I swaggered into Starbucks like I owned the place. I gazed at Cheryl like I owned her. Naturally, under the spell of my James Dean-esque look, Cheryl immediately weakened, softened, and became extremely vulnerable. At least, that's how I saw it. I gave the briefest hint of a smile. It was time. I strapped on my air guitar and launched into my version of the Beatles' "With A Little Help From My Friends":

What would you do if I cooked you a meal,
Would you sit down and eat it with me?
Lend me your pen; I'll give you my address
And I swear I'll cook low-calorie,
Oh, I cook Thai when seducing my friends,
Oh, you will sigh when our hot evening ends . . .

As Cheryl dashed out of Starbucks, she actually left a smoke trail behind her. I was both impressed and depressed.

Date #2: I entered Louise's Trattoria with enough rock star confidence for three women, but tonight it would be just me and Beverly, who appeared to be a classy woman. So I quickly decided on my own version of a timeless Broadway song, "Wouldn't It Be Loverly?" from *My Fair Lady*:

All I want is a girlfriend who
Is cute, funny, and Jewish, too,

Prefers blintzes to pork stew,
Oh, could she please be Beverly?

Beverly excused herself, suddenly remembering her 7:30 p.m. hair appointment, and dashed out. I was impressed that a hair salon stayed open so late on a Sunday night.

Date #3: Obviously, I needed to be more current in my song selections. So when I met Joan for a glass of wine at the M Bar, I slid next to her, smooth as Kanye West, took her hand, and sensually whisper-sang into her ear my version of the rap or hip-hop (like I would know the difference) song that won an Oscar, "It's Hard Out Here For a Pimp":

You know it's hard out here for a Jew,
When he's tryin' to find a woman who'll be true,
For the restaurant and Starbucks money spent,
I now don't have enough to pay my rent . . .

Joan vanished so quickly, I didn't even notice her leaving. Must have used some kind of futuristic, *Matrix*-like technology. But life is a learning experience, and I learned from my latest adventures at D.U. to stop trying to be something I'm not. As much as it pains me to admit it, I am not a rock star and most likely will never be one. I'm not even a polka star. And if I really want the kind of passion and devotion shown by groupies to their rock stars, I will simply have to earn it by being the very best me I can be. Now *there's* a challenge.

Perhaps I could get some perspective from my past girl-friends. That's always a good idea.

The Ghosts of Girlfriends Past

ne of the loneliest, most challenging activities and times of day for us singles is climbing into that big empty bed, late at night, all alone. Yet even when I don't have a current romantic partner, I'm never alone at night in my bed. No, it's not the triplets from the escort service. That gets old fast and, as it turns out, my charm wasn't the deciding factor in getting them to see me again. Nor is it the blow-up doll. That's in the shop for repair. I'm not alone because joining me are the living memories of my past failed relationships. Think of them as the singles version of the ghosts of Christmas past. On cold, dark nights, I can almost hear their plaintive cries echoing off my walls: "We need to talk" . . . "I love you but I'm not in love with you" . . . "It's not you; it's me" . . . "What was I thinking?" . . . "Oh, would you mind shutting the door on your way out?"

If you're already feeling so down that you can't even get a date, much less a lover, you need something to bolster your self-esteem. And what better for that than nightly visits from the ghosts of failed relationships past? You can relive, over and over again, in excruciating detail, every sad example of how you blew it romantically, which is why, after all, you're now alone, climbing into that seven mile-wide bed with the only person you've ever been able to please, the only person who truly understands you, the only person willing to put up with your many flaws and inadequacies—yourself.

Just to prove to yourself that your inability to maintain a lasting relationship with a woman is not a random thing, but that it is, in fact, a lifelong pattern of behavior, the evening's first ghost/memory of relationships past is invariably one of your earliest, prepubescent relationships—say, Diane Adelstein, an older woman. She was eight and I was seven. I was nuts about her, but the feeling wasn't mutual—a pattern that would repeat itself again and again throughout my dating life. Of course, when you're seven, there is no booze, drugs, therapists, or understanding male friends to help dull the pain. So instead of simply cutting my losses and walking away with a shred of dignity, I kept annoyingly trying to win Diane over until I eventually drove her to the point of calling me a jerk, an idiot, and a creep—to which I responded, and quite cleverly I thought in my seven-year-old mind, "Takes one to know one."

Ghost Diane fades to high school ghost Maureen. Truly lovely. So lovely, in fact, that I could not bring myself to even approach her. I felt unworthy. So I did the next best thing—the back of my house bordered the back of hers, and I watched her sunbathing through binoculars. Okay, so it wasn't a traditional romantic relationship, but for a lonely sixteen-year-old it was plenty romantic. And she only caught me once.

Ghost Maureen's glare lasts only momentarily until the Carol ghost appears. Carol, age twenty-two. Nonstop, steamy, sweaty, pulse-pounding sex for hours every day. Hey, come on, the law of averages says they can't all be dysfunctional disappointments.

I try to concentrate on Ghost Carol for as long as possible, but she is usually edged out of my mind by either the Kelly or the Emily ghost. Kelly wanted someone with more income; Emily wanted someone more communicative. Occasionally, when I'm really in the mood for beating up on myself, the Kelly and Emily ghosts will hit it off and walk away together, arm in arm, bad-mouthing me and giggling as they're replaced by the next relationship that didn't work out.

A reasonable person might ask why I torment myself this way, night after night, with the ghosts of my failed relationships. I think it has something to do with that old joke about why you keep pounding your head against the wall—because it feels so good when you stop. When I wake up each morning, the ghosts are gone. It's a clean slate. I've reviewed and learned from my lifelong relationship mistakes the night before and am ready to face the new day and the day's new women fresh and with joyous optimism—to make some brand-new mistakes, have new relationship ghost scenes play out, and learn even more lessons about romance. It's my own singles version of *The Lion King*'s "Circle of Life." And I hope to get it right, eventually.

At least I now have no fear of committing to a woman. No, my problem is the exact opposite of that.

Speed Loving: Recipe for Disaster

Pssst . . . I have a confession to make, and I have to get it off my chest. Not only do I *not* have the typical male problem of an inability to commit to a romantic relationship, but I seem to have the exact opposite syndrome. You see, I commit way too often and too easily. Say I'm on a coffee date that appears to be going well. The woman is attractive. The conversation is intelligent, entertaining, and flows smoothly. You might think she's interested in me. I certainly do.

What I've come to realize about this sort of encounter is that she may or may not be interested in a second date. She could simply be enjoying a pleasant first meeting and if I pursue anything further, I can pretty much be guaranteed some version of "You're a great guy. It was really nice meeting you, but I just wasn't feeling the magic/chemistry/spark/ mojo, etc."

Before, however, we EVEN get to DESSERT, my mind is hard at work. I'm planning NOT JUST our second date, BUT ALSO booking her for events up to six months down the line, introducing her to my friends and family, picking out towels and dinnerware with her at Macy's, and, of course, in the ultimate grand gesture of imagined mutual love—purchasing adjoining gravestones with lyrics of "our song" on each. The song, naturally: "'Til There Was You."

You might say that love at first sight isn't just a rare occurrence for me; it's pretty much my default mode. By the end of any positive coffee date, the two of us are already in a committed relationship, at least in my mind. This raises four questions:

1. Why am I like this?
2. What am I going to do about it?
3. Why should you care?
4. What can you do if you have the same problem?

Okay, the third question's just rude, so I'm going to ignore it.

I started thinking hard about why I fall in love so rapidly, and I think it's part of my optimistic nature. I see my bed as half full rather than half empty. I make Love Lemonade out of lemons. And I simply take it for granted that any woman naturally likes me as much as I like her. I am often wrong. And I am almost always surprised when I am wrong.

I clearly needed a plan of attack to correct this behavior. I realized it wouldn't be easy because it's against my loving nature, but I knew I was going to have to stop being so naïve, stop wearing my heart on my sleeve, stop making assumptions about what's simply a pleasant onetime encounter.

I decide to put my desire to change to the test. The next coffee date I have is with a woman named Jan. Within the first five minutes I'm with her, I check off the all-important five attributes she clearly has: smart, funny, attractive, interesting, fun. So naturally, this somehow triggers the part of my brain that transports me to Nordstrom to pick out our sheets. And I'm wondering if we should use an Arial or a Times New Roman font on our wedding invitations. That's when the alarm goes off in my brain or libido or wherever it is that the loving is happening, and I try forcing myself to stop.

To do so, I engage in what Method actors refer to as Sense Memory. I recall my marriage—how it started (a comedy series) and what it became (a cancelled drama). I flash forward my relationship with Kathy to the point that we're both fed up with one another and want out. This slows my libido way down. I immediately drop the bed sheets, walk out of Nordstrom, and settle into the more reasonable, mature perspective that Jan is a lovely woman with whom things may or may not work out for the long term and that it may take several dates, weeks, or even months to determine whether she is The One. My marriage may have failed, but its lessons will help me succeed.

So, what can I offer you, fellow post-divorce speed lovers? How about the other nine of the Ten Post-Divorce Dating Commandments, along with the one mentioned above?

I. Thou shalt be gun-shy about falling in love again.

II. Thou shalt slow down. Way down.

III. Thou shalt not let feelings in thy sexual parts overrule those in thy thinking parts.

IV. Thou shalt not assume the object of thy desire feels the same about thee.

V. Thou shalt not introduce her to thine parents/friends/children/neighbors/boss/co-workers within the first month of meeting her/him.

VI.   Thou shalt not purchase expensive gifts for her/
       him within the first month of meeting her/him.

VII.   Thou shalt not end thy memberships to online dating
       services within the first month of meeting her/him.

VIII. Thou shalt not suggest dating exclusivity within
       the first week of meeting her/him.

IX.   Thou shalt not utter the words "I love thee" during
       the first month of meeting her/him.

X.   If he/she chooses to end the brief "relationship,"
       thou shalt refrain from anything resembling a ner-
       vous breakdown.

The next time you see me, if I mention I'm in love, ask me how long I've been seeing her. If it's less than a month, slap my face and shout, "Snap out of it!" You have my permission.

Perhaps I could get my mind off of my propensity to fall in love quickly by instead focusing on devoting myself to serving others. Doesn't that sound noble?

Special Delivery

A nyone who denies that dating is every bit as time-consuming and soul-sucking as a regular job is either married or has gotten incredibly lucky in the dating universe. Or he's in prison, where romantic relationships take on a whole new perspective.

For the rest of us, however, it's Dating Apocalypse Now—and maybe forever—traveling on a patrol boat up a river through a romantic jungle. It's a perilous mission, fraught with lions and tigers and Claires, oh my.

For years, I'd been giving my second job, dating, an over-abundance of weight in my life, going all out to meet the right woman and make an impression, worrying about how she'd perceive my clothing, job, car, physical appearance, accomplishments, voice, ad dating infinitum.

Then, one day, I make e-mail and phone contact with Pamela, a woman who seems far less concerned with any of those—at least to her—superficial things. She doesn't even exercise her option for me to buy her dinner, lunch, a glass of wine, or a cup of coffee. What she does suggest for our first meeting is that I join her for her weekly Sunday morning activity: delivering bags of donated groceries to homebound men who have AIDS. Immediately, the usual first-date dilemmas—like which Frappucino drink to order—are rendered inconsequential.

We meet Sunday morning at a restaurant/soup kitchen on Fairfax, where we're given numerous bags of groceries and a sheet of six addresses in the Hollywood and Santa Monica areas. Pamela and I bring the bags of groceries to the men's homes, where they meet us at the door. They appear to be in various stages of health, ranging from very weak, with lesions on their necks and faces, to completely healthy-looking. We make awkward small talk with them, trying to keep things positive, asking one about his cat we see behind him, another about the colorful flowers outside his door. Some are more talkative than others; all are polite and grateful.

As we drive from one home to another, I think about the things in life that are so much more pressing and important than my dating desires—matters of actual life and death. Of course, they had always been there in the back of my mind, but to meet them head-on was very powerful. How minute my personal dating checklist seemed in this scheme of things.

Yet at the same time, I'm almost embarrassed to admit that I was feeling even more attracted to Pamela because of her humanitarian bent. She had revealed in herself a very good side, a perspective one could have only inferred over dinner or coffee. What other virtues might she have? Was I displaying a similarly virtuous side, and if so, did she feel the same way about me? Because if Starbucks is out and volunteering is in, if we're both truly the kind of people who see the value in doing something selfless, imagine the good we could do for each other.

Okay, so I'm not totally selfless. In fact, while Pamela and I were discussing volunteering and charity, I'll admit I was imagining us having our way with each other under a Greenpeace banner. But that's OK because we saved the world a little first. And if you can save the world a little and love somebody a little, well, that's a pretty good day.

Of course, a successful romantic relationship requires more in common from two people than simply their agreement about the value of humanitarian work. That's what Pamela and I discovered on our second date at a Japanese restaurant. Over tempura and teriyaki, whatever chemistry and rapport we'd had during our first date dissipated for no particular reason, slowly, like smoke into the sky. We both saw it leave. That is not an unusual occurrence for a couple within the first few dates. In fact, it's probably more the norm. In the past, I might have been frustrated by the disappointing outcome. But the only thing on my mind as I drove home that night was that whatever happens, even if the next twelve Starbucks dates take me deeper into the jungle, each day is a gift. And I could not wait to get back on that patrol boat.

But enough about me. Let's focus, at least momentarily, on the romantic fortune of my friends. And how that makes me feel.

Don't You Feel Happy When Your Friend Finds True Love?

Don't you feel happy when a friend of yours finds true love? I don't. I find it irritating. And I know what you're thinking: He's just jealous of anyone else having better romantic luck than he has. Hey, that's beside the point. OK, at least let me explain.

It all started when my friend Tanya called to say she had hit the romantic jackpot. After many years of trying, she finally found Mr. Right. She's absolutely thrilled with him and the feeling is mutual. She never realized love could be this fabulous. In fact, she doesn't even know what she was thinking before, being in relationships that were a mere shadow of this one's brilliance.

I expressed my happiness for her, hung up, and plunged into the throes of depression. I realized that I'd never experienced the highs of a relationship that Tanya described.

In fact, I was starting to suspect that that kind of perfect relationship did not exist in real life—maybe in the movies or in songs or on *Friends*, but that's it. And now Tanya had to spoil it all by finding perfect love right out here in the actual world. So, naturally, on my next coffee date, I'm sitting across from Linda and we're chatting, having a pleasant time. She's an attractive, interesting woman.

And then something rather unusual occurs. As we chat, my romantic soul, let's call him Alfonso, disengages himself from the rest of my body and floats overhead. Alfonso looks down on the scene, displeased. Why displeased? Because that infernal Tanya has raised the bar so high on what the perfect love relationship can be and, in Alfonso's eyes, should be. Alfonso informs me that, however pleasant, such perfection simply is not happening below.

I start arguing with Alfonso. Come on, Linda is a perfectly lovely woman. A professional. Attractive. Seems to appreciate me. I possibly could be happy with her. Maybe even forever.

But that's not good enough for Alfonso. Oh, no. He flings cold water in my face, cooling any ardor for Linda that was there before. He tells me to face the facts—she's just not soul mate material. There are no fireworks, no bells and buzzers going off. If Tanya's new relationship is a ten, this one's barely an eight. Alfonso puts it to me plainly: Am I going to be happy with an eight on the Perfect Relationship Scale, knowing Tanya is enjoying a ten every day for the rest of her life?

Now I'm getting angry. What makes you think, I ask Alfonso, that my present eight with Linda couldn't develop into a ten? It's our first meeting, for crying out loud. Alfonso tells me not to be a sap. He says I know good and well that if it's not here from the start, it never will be.

This really irks me. I accuse Alfonso of trying to undermine my chances for happiness. Suddenly, Linda notices that I am in midargument with what appears to be some imaginary thing over my head. She remembers an appointment she's late for, thanks me for the coffee, and quickly exits.

I do a slow burn, turning to face my romantic soul, who appears to be barely concealing a grin. Happy now, Alfonso? He tells me it was all for the best, and when I start moving toward him with my fist clenched, he reminds me that he's merely a part of me, so if I intend to do him any harm, I'm merely hurting myself.

Although I snap back that he's got a smart answer for everything, I realize he's right. Still, I'm seriously considering taking out a restraining order against him, and I'm trying my best these days to think positive thoughts about Tanya and her great new relationship. But man, it's a struggle.

Perhaps by now you're sensing that all the dating I've been doing has been getting to me. Am I doing too much of it? I mean, it's not that I've become addicted to dating. Have I? Why are you looking at me like that?

Do I Need a 12-Step Program for Serial Daters?

I s there a 12-step program for daters? If so, sign me up for DA—Date-aholics Anonymous. Not, mind you, that I'm addicted to dating. To me, dating is only a means to an end. I can stop any time I want to. No, really. I'm just using it. Having my way with it. Then, when I find my soul mate, I'll kick dating to the curb like an expired carton of milk. But I'm spending so much time and energy dating that it sometimes feels like an addiction. Or at least another career. If only it paid. And didn't involve so much time at Starbucks. And didn't require at the end of each meeting having to come up with a polite way to say, "It's perfectly okay with me if we never see each other again for the rest of our lives; in fact, I'd prefer it." Which usually emerges from my careful-to-be-tactful mouth in this fashion: "Very nice meeting you."

In the first three years following my divorce, I went on 150 dates. And by dates I'm using the standard *Merriam-Webster* dictionary definition: "first-time meetings, usually ending in disappointment." And I'm an optimist, mind you. Now, I realize that

150 dates sounds like a lot, but spread out over three years, it's just one a week. Of course, depending on the person, fifteen minutes with the wrong person for the first time can *seem* like one week. But I learned something very important from those 150 dates. I learned that if I had saved all the money I spent on them, I could have afforded a Hyundai. Granted, four of the dates resulted in relationships. But 146 of them resulted in: "Very nice meeting you." And a thorough knowledge of the differences between lattes, Frappuccinos, chais, and caramel macchiatos. If only that paid.

Sometimes I think this dating odyssey is God's way of getting back at me for never having taken chemistry in school. He's making it virtually impossible for me to find chemistry with my potential soul mate. Is mutual worship and adoration too much to ask? Of course not. You can ask for it all you want. Getting it—now that's the trick. Either they're not attracted to me or I'm not attracted to them. Sometimes they show up without a sense of humor, without a sense of playfulness, without even the realization that someone else is sitting across the table from them. They'll talk for a full hour about themselves without asking me one question about myself. Astounding. But at least they're setting their red flags up on the table right from the start. And for that I thank them.

I do like the variety, though. I've gone out with a judge, a cantor, a masseuse, a teacher, a network executive, a nurse, a college student, a speech therapist, a doctor, an actress, a psychologist, a lawyer, and even a forest ranger. I've had a first date in an art museum that featured life-sized, anatomically correct male and female mannequins. One date, as soon as we sat down to brunch, removed a digital scale from her pocketbook and proceeded to weigh each item of food that was served. At one Starbucks, I sat waiting an extra half hour for my date to arrive, even though she was already seated a few tables away, because she looked so different from her profile's photo that I could not believe that this was the same person. Finally, I approached her and she confirmed that she was, in fact, my date. Though to this day I remain unconvinced that she was not my date's mother.

Remember that *Seinfeld* episode where Jerry gets in trouble for being spotted making out with his date during *Schindler's List*? A recent date suggested, as a first date, that we see *The Pianist*, another Holocaust-themed movie. Beautifully done, very powerful and moving, but somehow doesn't quite set the desired mood for kicking off a romantic relationship. Oh, sure, I did what I could to salvage the mood afterward, with such comments as, "My apartment's in much better shape than that labor camp," but to no avail.

And though I've done my share of rejecting, I've also experienced my share of being rejected. At first, I'd take it personally. Now I consider it part of the process. Often, women can't bring themselves to say, "Sorry, not interested" to my face, so they'll lie. In one case, when I asked about the possibility of a next date, she responded, cheerfully, "Call me!" I did and never heard back from her. Now when I hear a cheerful "Call me!" I realize it's the kiss of death, not unlike that given by Michael Corleone in *The Godfather*. My favorite kiss-off, though, happened recently. I brought up the subject of a third date and actually heard these words come from her lips, "I'm going to be really busy in December." Wouldn't a quick slap across my face and knee to the groin have made the point more directly?

Then there are the ones who haven't quite mastered the tactful means of breaking off a long-term relationship. To my mind, there's just one way to do it right—face-to-face, honestly, acknowledging the person's wonderful qualities and the great times had together. The wrong ways—disappearing without a word, doing it over the phone, e-mailing a "Dear John" letter, sending big brother Sonny Corleone to bounce some metal garbage pails off my head. Okay, that last one hasn't happened. Yet. But, come on, ladies, acknowledge the good. And act like a human being. And if they're open to it, I enjoy staying in touch with them even after the relationship is over. In some ways, you can become even better friends—with the added bonus of hearing about all their subsequent dysfunctional relationships.

So why go through all the pain, the aggravation, the expense, the wasted time, the same interview-like questions, over and over again? The singles websites, the speed dating, singles events, personals ads, blind dates, dates, matchmaking services, friend setups. Am I masochistic? Am I a serial dater so addicted to the process that I consciously or subconsciously never intend to settle down with one of them? I don't think so.

I'll tell you why I go through it all and why I'll continue to go through it all. It's because I've experienced a relationship when it works. In fact, I've been lucky enough to have had more than one relationship in which both people worshipped and adored one another. Now, I'm guessing that for most people these kinds of relationships don't happen often. But when they do, it's special, exciting, stimulating, life-enhancing. It's magic. And I know she's out there somewhere, perhaps even looking for me. All I ask is that at the end of our first date, she doesn't look me in the eyes and say, cheerfully, "Call me!" At least give me a chance at honesty, before I'm left to drown in a dating ocean so vast that it renders any sense of navigation fruitless.

Part C: Help! I'm Drowning in the Dating Ocean!

I've Had 500 Dates—Kill Me Now

I have a confession and a request. My confession: I have experienced approximately 500 dates. That's right—I have had a one-date connection with 500 women. My request: Kill me now.

Remember the controversy the United States endured over its practice of waterboarding political prisoners at Guantanamo Bay to force confessions out of them? How it was said to be cruel and unusual punishment? Well, as a result of that controversy, waterboarding has been discontinued. Instead, political prisoners are now forced to go on dates. Which I personally believe constitutes even crueler and more unusual punishment. But the Obama Administration didn't check with me before instituting that policy.

As a result now, often when political prisoners are informed that they will be made to go on a coffee date, their typical response is, "No, please! For the love of Allah, I'll talk! I'll tell you everything! Here's a map indicating where the weapons of mass destruction are hidden! Here are the home addresses of the most powerful al-Qaida leaders! Just, please, no dates! I beg you!"

Before proceeding, perhaps I should define dates for those of you unfamiliar with them. And why would you be unfamiliar with dates? Perhaps you've never had to go on one. Darn you! Perhaps you met your soul mate in high school or college and have been in a committed relationship ever since. Darn you! Perhaps you're a member of a religious order where you're in a committed relationship to God, who apparently requires no dates. Darn you!

But back to the definition. A coffee date is simply a first-time, in-person meeting with a potential romantic partner (PRP), usually over coffee, usually resulting from initial online contact over one of the online dating sites such as Match.com, and usually resulting in the Three D's: disappointment, depression, and despair. A coffee date is not unlike a job interview, except your date doesn't validate your parking and usually doesn't ask for an example of how you prioritize and deal with multiple deadlines.

As you might imagine, having logged 500 dates, I have consumed what scientists refer to in technical terminology as "a buttload of caffeine." Consequently, I've been unable to fall asleep for the past nine years. I am exhausted.

In addition, because I live in Los Angeles, one encounters a number of women desirous of money, fame, and power. Since I have none of those, I've been forced to rely upon the poor substitutes of intelligence, personality, and charm—which for some L.A. women, clearly marks me as handicapped. But I'm not bitter.

Of course, you may be wondering, especially those of you who've never been on a coffee date, *Mark, these dates of which you speak frankly don't sound so bad. After all, they're just a half hour to an hour meeting with someone who could very well turn out to be your LRP (Lifelong Romantic Partner), your soul mate. Sounds exciting and romantic, Mark, so why are you asking us to kill you now?*

"Exciting and romantic"? Oh, you poor, misguided creatures. A typical coffee date is exciting and romantic in the same way that a colonoscopy is soothing and carefree. But allow me to preface my complaints by saying that obviously they're coming from a person who has experienced the entire gamut of dates—the good, the bad, and the ugly. I feel as though I've lived several lifetimes in my 500 dates. It's practically a form of immortality—but without the impressive entry in the *Encyclopaedia Brittanica* or even Wikipedia.

Okay, I can see it in your eyes. You want specifics. You want the specifics? You can't handle the specifics! But I'll give 'em to you anyway. I've had dates who've never even showed up. They forget the day or time, or something or someone better comes up. Or she shows up looking more like the *mother* of the woman in her posted photo. Some spend the entire coffee date talking solely about themselves without asking me one thing about myself. Please explain that one to me.

One woman actually took out a small digital food scale and proceeded to weigh each item of her lunch. When I expressed surprise, she assured me that all of her girlfriends do it. Even when they go out to eat in a group with their various boyfriends and husbands, she told me, the guys'll be at one end of the table talking their guy stuff and the gals at the other end, just chatting away and weighing their food.

Granted, some of my dates have been considerate enough to present their red flags right from the start. One of them lived with her mother, had no car, and suffered from about five unusual medical conditions. Another admitted she was fifteen years older than the age she'd stated on her dating profile. When she saw that that bothered me, she accused me of being superficial.

One date showed up in her forest ranger uniform and appeared stocky enough to bench-press me and 500 pounds extra. Another woman made out with me for half an hour and the next day e-mailed me that she wasn't interested in meeting again because she didn't feel the chemistry was there. Another woman with deadly food allergies carried a hypodermic needle filled with adrenaline for me to inject into her should she go into anaphylactic shock.

I don't want to give you the idea that all the weird and negative stuff came exclusively from the women I dated. Because I'm equally guilty and would like to confess to a number of sins:

- I've had sex way too soon before really getting to know them
- I've given up on relationships way too soon
- I've stayed in relationships way too long
- I've coveted my neighbor's wife (And that's one of the Ten Commandments, so I'm not counting on getting into Heaven)
- I've also coveted my friend's wife, my neighbor's daughter, my friend's daughter, my first cousin, my second cousin, my third cousin, and a woman in the Macy's catalog bra ad who was definitely one half to one third of my age and I should be ashamed of myself

You'd think with all the dating experience I've had on these sites, I'd get better at it, show steady improvement . . . at least not repeat the same mistakes. You'd be wrong. The only conclusion I've come to in matters of the heart is that you just never know. Every person is different. Every relationship is different. And if you're lucky, you'll meet someone with whom you'll just click. And that will make all the rejection, all the chase, all the disappointment, effort, and heartbreak of the past worthwhile. The romantic payoff.

So, on second thought, if I may, I'm changing my mind. Don't kill me now. Give me some encouragement. Tell me a love story of your own—or about someone you know. Give me the push and the strength and the inspiration to continue the quest.

That way, the next time I'm seated across the table from my Match.com coffee date whom I've already realized in the first ten minutes is completely wrong for me, I'll smile, realizing I'm one person closer to finding my soul mate. I will be patient. So, even if she turns out to be a forest ranger with a broccoli allergy who weighs her food and lives with her mother—so be it. I won't complain. She can even bench-press me. As long as she likes the Beatles and chocolate. I mean, a man has to have *some* standards.

At the very least, we can be honest with each other. Which got me to thinking—what if on our first dates, we were absolutely honest with each other? Yikes!

Coffee Date's Hidden Thoughts—Revealed!

n a typical coffee date, because we're meeting for the first time, awkward conversation comes with the territory. Neither of us completely reveals what we're thinking or feeling. We're shy, holding back, concealing, putting on a good face, feeling the other person out.

How much more interesting the first date would be if we both were to communicate our true emotions! Still, those actual thoughts and feelings are definitely present, whether uttered or not. They're simply bubbling under the conversation's surface. Biding their time until we feel more comfortable and trusting with one another.

For instance, take this (nearly) verbatim transcript from one of my dates. All unuttered thoughts have been italicized for the protection of the emotionally fragile.

Me: Renee?

Here I go again. Date #163, but who's counting? At this rate, by next May, I'll have dated every unattached woman in the country. At which time I'll have to start importing them from other countries and taking Berlitz classes.

Renee: Hi, Mark. Nice to meet you.

Dear Lord, please don't let this one be a stalker, a jerk, or have serious psychological issues like the last six. I believe I've reached my annual quota for restraining orders.

Me: Should we get some coffee and sit down?

And then decide within ten minutes whether there's a chance we might eventually see each other naked, or, and most likely, never see each other again?

Renee: Sounds good.

Looks like I'm gonna have to train this one how to dress, make eye contact, speak, stand up straight, and do something with that hair. Yep, this one's a definite fixer-upper. Again. Dear Lord, just shoot me now.

Me: So, have you been doing this Internet dating thing long?

Exactly how many guys have you rejected, and how many have rejected you? Be specific. You have five minutes to answer. Show all work. Begin.

Renee: You're actually the first coffee date I've been on.

Today. The sum total of all my dates could fill Dodger Stadium. And it's always I who do the rejecting because I am perfect and they are flawed. Capiche? So unless your own perfection level approaches mine, you might as well start heading over to the stadium right now.

Me: What are you looking for in a relationship?
Are you a) high-maintenance? b) emotionally needy? c) nuts?

Renee: Oh, I don't know. I guess the usual—chemistry, shared goals, friendship.
A man with Brad Pitt's looks and Bill Gates's bank account who can make me yodel in bed. That specific enough for you, Sparky?

Me: What kinds of things do you like to do for fun?
And please, know that the Red Flag Alert goes up immediately with any hint of chick flicks, shopping, or eating at restaurants whose names begin with a "Le."

Renee: I'm pretty down-to-earth. Just the usual.
That is, if you define "usual" as a) frequent "Where is this heading?" talks about our relationship b) having my mother visit us as often as possible c) making it my lifelong mission to interest you in ballet and opera.

Me: Is it just me, or am I sensing some chemistry here?
I'm picturing you without your clothing right now, but I'm gonna have to do some up-close-and-personal research in order to get the full effect.

Renee: You might be right.
It's just you.

Me: May I walk you to your car?

And check out your rear view as I, the perfect gentleman, allow you to walk in front of me?

Renee: Sure. Can I contribute something to the bill?
And need I remind you that a "yes" answer on your part will forever brand you as a cheapskate of the highest caliber?

Me: Oh, no, I've got it. Thanks.
I accepted one of those invitations to contribute once before and ended up as the featured newcomer on www.cheapdates-toavoid.com for two months.

Me: Well, here we are. It was really good to meet you.
Because I enjoy taking two-hour chunks out of my day to spend time with people I'll never see again.

Renee: You, too. You seem like a really nice guy.
And we'll have our next date when Lindsay Lohan becomes a nun.

On second thought, perhaps those dates are better off with the actual thoughts and feelings remaining bubbling under the conversation's surface. After all, if you start off a romantic relationship with absolute honesty, no telling what madness and chaos would result.

Damn You, Foundation of Friendship!

Get this. At least six different times, I've had dates with the same type of woman—one who has had a long history of wild, impulsive, passionate, no-holds-barred sex. She invariably finds something lacking in that lifestyle and decides to make a change. Starting with the very next man she dates. Who is invariably me. Or, grammatically, is it I? Either way, she tells one of us that I will not, in contrast to her sordid past, become the beneficiary of her uninhibited passions. No. With me, things will be different. Rather than her typical rushing into sex, she will hold out—and thus I will have to hold out—until she feels that we have established that all-important . . . (DRUMROLL) . . . Foundation of Friendship. Which will make the intimacy all the more special and long-lasting once it occurs. Don't I agree?

Let me recreate one of these six magical conversations— or, better, monologues—that I've experienced. Share my pain: "Mark, I'm really flattered that you find me attractive enough to want to become intimate. I'm very attracted to you, too. And in the past, it wouldn't have been unusual for me to jump into bed with a guy on the first, second, or third date. And, don't get me wrong—I love sex and am a very passionate and giving lover. I crave sex. But where are all those guys I had sex with? Obviously, not in the picture anymore. The only thing I have from them are my memories of the endless hot, steamy, sheet-drenched love-making. But I'm so over that now. It's just not enough. I want and need a substantial, committed, lasting relationship. Which I know will not happen if we have sex right away. Look, I care about you. I want us to last. But for that to happen, and before we take our clothes off, it's important to me that we establish that all-important . . . (DRUMROLL) . . . Foundation of Friendship. Don't you agree?"

(SIGH) Jeez Louise, now I'm in a bind. If I disagree, she'll perceive me as some impatient, horny pig who doesn't care about her feelings or our romantic future. But if I agree, for the next three months I may as well be a eunuch.

I try to strike a reasonable middle ground, saying that although I agree with her new direction in principle, I have noticed from my own experience, for what it's worth, that the length of time I wait to have sex has little bearing on the relationship's subsequent longevity. Some of my longest-lasting relationships started off with a bang, so to speak; and some of my shortest ones didn't. But even before I get all the words out, I can see that her mind's made up, her legs are crossed, and for the next few months, the Pope and I will be sharing the exact same level of sexual activity.

Look, I don't mind being punished for my own mistakes and behavior. But I keep being punished for other people's lack of self-control and inhibitions. It's just not fair.

Finally, is a fulfilling romantic relationship too much to ask for?

I'm Not Asking for the Moon and the Stars

One of the greatest mysteries in my life, besides how to program my TiVo, is why it's taking me so long to meet my soul mate. After all, Los Angeles is filled with hundreds of thousands of women, maybe even millions, looking for their soul mate. And I've had dates with seemingly most of them. You'd think by now we would have run into each other. Perhaps we've passed each other on the way to dates with others who are wrong for us. That makes me sad.

Granted, I did not appear in *People* magazine's most eligible bachelors issue—I guess they didn't receive my photo by press time. Still, what am I, chopped liver? I've got all my vital limbs and organs. Original teeth. Original hair. Fairly decent personal hygiene habits. Gainfully employed. Far more attractive than the Elephant Man. And capable of cooking an omelet in a single bound. Take *that*, Orlando Bloom!

So, what is it? Am I being too picky? I don't think so. I mean, it's not like I'm asking for the moon and the stars. My place doesn't have room for them anyway. All I want is someone who's reasonably attractive, preferably brunette, not yet collecting Social Security, with a slender to athletic figure, who's a nonsmoker eats healthily, exercises regularly, has a sense of humor, and lives with fewer than nine cats. There should be a few women like that in Los Angeles, wouldn't you think?

Of course, as with any fully-evolved human being, I'd expect her to be optimistic, enthusiastic, energetic, and creative—not to mention considerate, affectionate, and passionate. And, of course, I wouldn't say no if she turned out to be giving, flexible, romantic, spontaneous, and communicative. Considering the fact that this person will hopefully be my life partner, is all that really too much to ask? I'm even willing to help with the intensive training on the affectionate and passionate parts.

All the above qualifications would naturally be the absolute minimum I'd expect for her to even be in the ballpark of consideration, which is located just a few miles from the soccer fields of possibility. Additional icing-on-the-cake qualities might include trust, commitment, sensitivity, intellectual curiosity, and a love of intimacy. Aren't these things everyone wants and deserves? I mean, come on, folks, this is basic Relationship 101 stuff, isn't it? Hello? Operator, I think I've been cut off!

OK, so you tell me. Am I being absolutely out of line to expect my romantic partner to enjoy Chinese, Indian, Italian, Japanese, Mexican, Thai, and vegetarian food? Is it crazy to think she should be fond of big band, swing, classic rock, classical, folk, blues, and rock music? Am I really stretching things to expect that she'll join me in biking, bowling, hiking, jogging, swimming, tennis, and weight lifting? And that she won't say no to movies, plays, bookstores, comedy clubs, poetry slams, museums, concerts, walks, and exploring ethnic restaurants and festivals?

Level with me, please. Am I being outrageously unrealistic in having these kinds of expectations? And please don't misunderstand—I'm not looking for a carbon copy of myself, just someone who shares most of my interests and traits and beliefs about a romantic relationship. It's not like I'm not flexible or don't accept people's differences. If she doesn't enjoy playing Scrabble, that's fine. She probably has some hobby or interest that I'm not into, as well—such as Parcheesi or the Republican Party. As long as she's Jewish.

Look, even if my potential soul mate has just 50 percent of the above attributes, I'd be thrilled and consider myself very lucky. And I can't help but noticing that that percentage figure seems to be shrinking as time marches on. Catch me in five years and it should be down to 10 percent. Five years after that—if she's breathing and female, it'll be A-OK with me. Okay, forget all of the above. I'm basically looking for someone who's nuts about me, and vice versa. And if she turns out to be a Tibetan yak herder obsessed with barbecued pork and Yoko Ono music—well, hell, she's my dream girl!

What's a guy have to do to get a girlfriend, write her a letter even if he hasn't yet met her? Hey, at this point, I was ready to try anything.

A Letter to My Future Soul Mate

ear Future Soul Mate,

Forgive me for not using your actual name. You see, we haven't met yet. Tell you what— how 'bout I just refer to you as Julie? I've always liked that name, and I wouldn't be surprised if you ended up having it. Y'know, it feels strange expressing my deepest personal thoughts to a woman I haven't even seen, but I'm making an exception for you because, after all, we will eventually be together for the rest of our lives. Plus, just because we haven't met yet, that doesn't mean we can't share our feelings, right? This way, when we finally do meet, we'll be that much farther along in the relationship. It'll be like our seventh date. Just think of the intimacy.

After many years of not being able to find you, Julie—well, two years to be exact, the frustration of the endless search started to get to me. It seemed like I was right on track for turning into the male equivalent of the old spinster with seven cats and a passion only for crocheting sweaters for friends and relatives (and their pets) lucky enough to have found relationships. I felt myself beginning to experience the Seven Stages of No Soul Mate Grief.

First, there was Shock—the horrifying realization that we may never meet. It seemed as though every woman I met had a giant neon NOT YOUR SOUL MATE sign atop her head. Oh, sure, some of them were attracted to me, and it wouldn't have been difficult to have comforted myself with a series of meaningless, superficial sexual encounters. But that's not what I wanted; that's not me. Ultimately, that's not even satisfying, in case my mother is reading this.

Denial followed shock. All evidence to the contrary, Julie, I informed anyone who asked about it, that it was simply a question of time and luck before I'd meet my soul mate. Those to whom I'd say this would nod and give me a half-smile, attempting to be supportive, but, oh yes, I could see the pity in their eyes. It was the exact same look my parents gave me when I informed them that rather than going to law school, I was going to give stand-up comedy a try.

As I moved into the Bargaining stage, I attempted to cope with my loss of soul mate hope by making a deal with God. "Lord, if You allow me to meet my soul mate, I'll become a better person. I'll attend temple more often; I'll be kinder to people; I'll make donations to charity even if they don't send the personalized, self-sticking address labels; I'll stop taking your name in vain when the driver in front of me is too slow to make it through the yellow light; I'll subscribe to PBS. I'll floss."

Of course, the Guilt stage was no big shocker to me, as I was quite experienced in that arena. It took the form of multiple "if only"s. If only all the relationship wisdom I'd read about and received from others had sunk in. If only I hadn't turned Kathy down just because when she laughed, she sounded like a goat. If only Pam hadn't caught me trying on her underwear. (Hey, come on, it was research. Okay, I was just curious. Oh, all right, it was a very stressful period in my life and there was no chocolate around.)

It's no wonder I reached the Anger stage. I was angry at life for forcing me to keep paying monthly fees to online dating websites rather than the much easier and far more economical method of simply accidentally bumping into my soul mate in an elevator or supermarket, with appropriate Phil Collins or Elton John soundtrack music, just like in the movies. I was angry at myself for not having developed whatever relationship skills might turn me into a babe magnet. I was angry at my parents for not having given me more superficial genetic gifts and fewer tendencies to self-analyze.

Depression followed closely upon Anger, Julie. Look what you did to me, and you didn't even know me. I lost interest in dating at all, much less meeting my soul mate. I sounded as though all the life and energy had been drained from my voice. I slumped. I couldn't even motivate myself to call a depression hotline. And here's how I realized I was truly, deeply depressed—I watched daytime TV. Three days in a row. Do you know how deeply depressed a man has to be to watch daytime TV?

Finally, I became resigned to the fact that some people just aren't meant to meet their soul mates and apparently I was one of them—the few, the lonely, the man doomed for the rest of his life to face a restaurant maitre d' who, while the Muzak is playing Roy Orbison's "Only the Lonely," looks at him pityingly and asks, "Table for one?" and then shines a spotlight on him as all eyes follow him to his solitary table, offering looks of sympathy as the waiter removes one of the place settings and he finally cries out in anguish, "Please, for the love of God, look away. I am alone and hideous!"

So, how, you may wonder, did things turn out relatively well? How did I finally arrive at the last of the Seven Stages of No Soul Mate Grief—the stage of Acceptance and Hope? Well, Julie, you see, there's some good news. I met someone. Finally. Which to me pretty much constitutes proof of God's existence. The walking on water thing? Nah. Changing water into wine? Uh-uh. Finding a woman I like as much as she likes me? Bingo. And I really like her. I even got rid of all my chocolate for her. Well, not totally; it's wrapped securely in the third cabinet on the left. You never know.

Is this woman my soul mate, Julie? Who knows? At this point, I'm not even sure what it would feel like to have a soul mate. I mean, come on, her name isn't even Julie. Perhaps that's a red flag. It's just that . . . maybe if you find someone you really like, who seems to like you, is pretty and smart and doesn't seem to mind your flaws and smells good and doesn't even bring up the subject of restraining orders, that's soul mate enough for any man. Even me. Now, if you'll excuse me, Julie, I need to go floss and get ready for temple.

Best wishes,
Mark

And as long as I'm in an opening-up mood, allow me to share a painful dating experience with you. Misery loves company, so please, join me!

A Personal Invitation to Share My Dating Pain

Isn't relating to the opposite sex supposed to get easier over time? One develops certain techniques—charm, knowledge, experience, finesse. And one uses all that to make a positive impression on one's date. Makes perfect sense. So why isn't it working out that way for me? I seem to be no more savvy about male-female relationships than I was back in high school, several long-term relationships and one mangled marriage ago.

But perhaps something positive can be salvaged from my recent sad experience in the treacherous waters of the dating world. Perhaps my failure and heartbreak can serve as a cautionary warning to others. So, please, come along on my ill-fated singles journey, won't you? Share my pain. Read it and weep. Just promise me one thing—if you do learn anything from what follows, would you please let me know what it is? Because, frankly, I'm still baffled.

It started when I saw Kathy's photo on her online dating service profile. Her photo jumped out at me. Not literally—though I understand that technology's just a few years away. It wasn't a model-pretty face, like Julia Roberts's. It was warmer and more accessible, like, oh, like Marisa Tomei's. And I really like Marisa Tomei. Only Kathy's face had more character and a nicer smile. No offense, Marisa.

And the written portion of her profile was just perfect. The way she described herself was exactly what I wanted in a potential soul mate. And the traits she said she wanted in a man were ones I had. It was so obvious that we were made for each other. I had pleasurable visions of the dating search being over. At last, I had found my Kathy. Just one teeny little thing remained—seeing if she'd feel the same way.

Sometimes before everything collapses, God plays a little joke on you. He starts you off with a few positive experiences, just to get your hopes up. God was in a joking mood with me and Kathy. So when I contacted her, asking her to check out my profile and write back if interested, she wrote back, interested! I was king of the world! I literally danced around my apartment, singing joyfully. And I can't dance. Or sing. But I was Fred Astaire and Frank Sinatra that day.

We started e-mailing each other; the chemistry was easy and natural. And that chemistry transferred over to our phone conversation. I liked Kathy's voice, her energy, her style. I liked what she said and how she said it, and she seemed to be responding to me in kind. We decided to meet, and she chose a place near her for coffee. If you told me then I'd just won a multimillion-dollar lottery, I swear I wouldn't have been any more excited. So this is what it feels like when you finally locate your soul mate.

When I walked in, Kathy was there already. She was much prettier than her photo. We gave each other a hug and sat down. We ordered coffee and began to converse. Everything I'd felt about her before our meeting, I was feeling even more so. We gave each other compliments. We talked about being able to give up the nonstop singles profiles searching. We talked about one day being so close that we could cry in each other's arms. We held hands a little bit and sat next to each other and even had the waitress take our photo together. We made plans to see each other for date number two the very next night and gave each other warm hugs before saying goodbye.

I could honestly have died happily at that moment. So imagine my shock when later that night, I received this e-mail from Kathy:

"Thanks again for coming today to meet. You are a very funny and entertaining guy, and though I enjoyed talking with you, there are things I'm not comfortable with, and don't wish to explore it any further. I am absolutely certain you will meet your soul mate, and I will keep my eyes open, and won't feel shy to send someone your way."

After I semirecovered from the punch to the heart, I tried to think of what might have happened to change Kathy's mind. Did I come on too strong? Does she have intimacy issues? Did something I said or wrote offend her? Did an old boyfriend come back into the picture? I just didn't know. I e-mailed Kathy, but her answers were vague, and it soon became apparent that that ship had sailed; after one date, we were finished. I had gone through the entire arc of a relationship, from initial hope to final despair, and we'd only seen each other once.

This dating thing is one tough road. You spend so much time and energy looking for the right person, and when it seems that you've found her, a thousand things can happen to mess it up. Or one thing. So maybe I never will find my soul mate. Or maybe I'll have fifty more disappointing experiences before I do. But I have to believe she's out there. And I have to believe we'll find each other. And that things will work out when we do. Maybe at that point, I won't be king of the world. And maybe she won't look anything like Marisa Tomei. But I do know this—it will all have been worth it.

Which is not to say that there won't be bizarre surprises even after one acquires a girlfriend. Such as, for example, one's girlfriend and wife actually bonding!

Help! My Girlfriend and Ex-Wife Are Hitting It Off!

L ike most of your basic North American, garden-variety neurotics, I've experienced all your standard nightmares—from oversleeping for a crucial job interview to being trapped inside a car that's slowly sinking in the ocean. Yet nothing could have prepared me for the nightmare that one day suddenly presented itself in the course of my real, waking life—the anticipation of my girlfriend and ex-wife meeting for the first time. Cue musical sting.

Okay, so I was lucky enough to be in one of those rare periods of my dating life when I was seeing someone regularly. Why are you looking so surprised? We even called each other girlfriend and boyfriend. And normally, one's interaction with one's girlfriend is kept separate from one's dealings with one's ex-wife. But now, an opportunity had presented itself for those two very different worlds to collide.

Naturally, like the optimist I am—okay, the realist I am . . . oh, alright, the pessimist I am—I feared the worst. It all started, like most tales of terror do, with my ex-wife, Pauline (Names have been changed to protect those involved. Okay, to protect me), deciding to throw a New Year's Day open house dinner party to which she invited a selection of her friends, neighbors, and co-workers, our two kids, and, in a glorious display of mature, California-style open-mindedness and generosity—myself and my girlfriend of two months, Erin.

Of course, my initial reaction to this invitation was not, "Oh, what a glorious display of mature, California-style open-mindedness and generosity." It was: "All right, what's the catch? What's her motive? How will I invariably end up paying?" And then it was: "How can I get out of it?" and, failing that, "What's the worst that could happen if I went?"

The worst that could happen seemed obvious to me. I envisioned two possible scenarios. In the first, Pauline and Erin have at each other like rabid dogs, screaming insults, tearing hair, breaking furniture—which ends up on YouTube, courtesy of one of the guest's cell phone cameras. Our kids deal with this for years in therapy.

In the second scenario, during the party, while I excuse myself to deal with my nausea in the bathroom, Pauline would take Erin aside and present to her a list of all 273 of my failings, most of which, she confides to Erin, won't become noticeable until month three of Erin's being with me. Erin is stunned; she'd only been aware of 149 of my failings. Pauline places a compassionate arm around Erin's shoulder and whispers to her, "For the love of God, save yourself!" The next day, Erin leaves me.

Okay, so that's the worst that could happen. Now, how can I get out of it? The question is asked too late—I discover that Erin thinks it's a good and healthy idea for us to go. I'm stuck.

What actually happened wasn't quite so dramatic and not nearly as centered around me as I'd imagined. First off, at the party, Pauline was in her full Be Nice to New People mode. You know the one—where in order to make a good impression on someone you're meeting for the first time, you present yourself as a more polite, more considerate, more charming, and more entertaining version of your actual self. I remember thinking that if Pauline had been that version of herself during the marriage, we'd still be together. I was about to whisper to Erin, "Don't fall for it," when I couldn't help noticing that she was falling for it. Pauline was charming her.

The next thing I know, Erin and Pauline are yakking and cackling away like a couple of lifelong friends. They discussed their jobs, their health, our kids, life in general. They apparently weren't even talking about me. I'm pretty sure they forgot I was there. All right, I know what you're thinking: *That's all well and good, Mark, but what can I learn from it?* It's always about you, isn't it? Okay, look, here are the ABCs that I learned from my daymare—the daytime version of a nightmare.

A) Give yourself some credit. Give yourself some extra credit. If your significant others made it through all your various filters to the point that you were willing to marry/date them, perhaps you're more of a good judge of character than you think. Trust, therefore, that they'll have it within themselves to behave graciously.

B) Stop trying to control the situation or prevent it from happening. Let things take their own natural, organic course. Relax. Breathe into it. Have a sense of humor about it. Or borrow someone else's sense of humor for the day. (But return it in good condition.)

Writing is My Lady

So I'm having a Rat Pack moment one day, sipping a martini and listening to Frank Sinatra singing "L.A. Is My Lady," a song in which he uses the City of Angels metaphorically for his romantic relationships. Yeah, it's just a typical Thursday for me, when it strikes me that my own version of the Chairman of the Board's hit would be "Writing Is My Lady," Why writing? The fact is that the arc of the script-writing experience absolutely parallels that of a romantic relationship. No, really. So quit giving me the stink-eye.

The genesis of every great script is the same—finding that amazing idea, the one worthy of several months of the writer's time, multimillions of the studio's budget, and $12 and two hours of each audience member's life—give or take $35 for a large popcorn and a box of Milk Duds. Oh, sure, we writers can have dalliances with an array of perfectly adequate ideas, but the great idea, like the great romantic partner, is rare. Which is why when we encounter either one it feels like magic. And why they throw money at a good idea like Russell Crowe tossing a telephone at a hotel desk clerk's head—without fully thinking it through.

Naturally, we want to explore that magic. Find out everything we can about our idea, or about our romantic partner. Spend time with her, him, or it. Converse. Research. Run a background check. It's *The King and I's* "Getting To Know You" phase in which, whether it's a wonderful idea or an amazing romantic partner, I notice that I love everything and everyone. Yes, even you! Disgustingly sappy? Sure. But it's OK, 'cause I'm in love with a great idea or a great woman. So pour on the sap. It's chocolate to me, baby.

Once I've spent enough time in the cocooning phase with my new PSO (potential significant other), it's time for us to appear together in public as a couple—our coming out, as it were. Show ourselves off. Let the world know of our love. Similarly with the written idea—we take it out of the drawer, run it by our friends, neighbors, fellow writers for their feedback, hoping that they'll equally embrace our idea and romantic partner—though for them, singing Rogers & Hammerstein is completely optional.

If the feedback is positive at this stage, we up the stakes, taking the idea to the next level—agents, managers, development executives. This is potentially the most dangerous level because the idea can be killed here for any number of reasons: "It's derivative," "It's already in development," "Not commercial enough; it'll never sell." The equivalent danger territory here in romance is introducing our PSO to our family, whose negative response can cause the relationship plug to be pulled faster than Ricky Gervais being invited back again to host the Golden Globe Awards.

At a certain point, we push aside all our other writing projects—and dates—to focus exclusively on this one writing project—and date—that has so captivated us. Our friends have no need to ask what we're working on or whom we're seeing, because those ideas/PSOs are with us all the time. We eat, sleep and breathe them—which can't be healthy, but what choice do we have? We've become obsessed.

Yet obsession seldom lasts. Eventually, the initial flash of excitement over the script dims as we settle into the hard work of writing. The relationship's honeymoon period often ends as the couple deals with the day-to-day challenges and conflicts inherent in making any long-term relationship work, and the writer in making the script work. Finally, if we manage to solve all the script's major problems, we've truly bonded with it. We're engaged.

From there, it's smooth sailing 'til we finish the script, perhaps allowing ourselves the relief and joy of a celebration to acknowledge the important accomplishment. And likewise, of course, to acknowledge the completion of our life as a single person—the bachelor party.

And before we know it, we've entered the period of registering—at city hall for our marriage license, at Bloomingdale's for our wedding gifts, at WGA Script Registration for, well, you know. Registering the script gives us some degree of legal protection, just as the wedding makes our marriage legal.

At the subsequent wedding party, we appear for the first time in public together as husband and wife, fully registered, with all due legal protections. And when we walk into that movie lot office to pitch our registered script, we're also appearing, writer and script, as a newly committed couple.

Aah, this is the honeymoon period, in which the writer has not a care in the world, just every expectation of the ultimate in gratification—selling the script. Just as on your honeymoon when you might be offered drinks at poolside or on the beach, movie studio assistants offer the writer drinks before the pitch meeting. Okay, they're bottled waters, but they're still drinks.

And after each pitch session, the writer turns to his agent, manager, or writing partner and asks the equivalent of the honeymoon's, "Was it good for you, too?"

Invariably, as the pitches continue, instances of negativity rear their ugly little heads. Development executives point out weaknesses in story, character, theme, and dialogue. There's trouble in paradise at home, too. Just three short months ago, your blushing bride was referring to you as "Mister Perfect." Now, however, she is truly miffed that Mister Perfect: a) constantly leaves a snail-like trail of clothing, food, and newspapers throughout the house wherever he roams, b) can't stand her mother or most of her other relatives, for that matter, and c) somehow neglected to mention that he'd rather impale himself on a javelin than become a father.

Flash forward. Your script is rejected everywhere. Your agent informs you that your script is dead in the water. Your agent also informs you that you are dead in the water—and drops you from his client list. This coincides, of course, with your wife filing for divorce. So, suddenly, you're unmarried, unrepresented, miserable, and convinced that you will never again find someone to love or success as a writer. Days, months, or years go by. Then, one day, you meet this really cool woman . . . and get this really exciting idea for a movie . . .

So, yes, writing is indeed my lady. It's every writer's lady—or gentleman, depending on your preference. I've been through all these stages with both my women and my writing, and I definitely have a love-hate relationship with both. In fact, just thinking about it suddenly gives me writer's block.

One of my writing teachers suggested a way to work through writer's block and make the writing better—raise the stakes. Perhaps that's what this next date tried to do with me for her own dating efforts. Boy, did she raise the stakes.

I Was a Woman's Last Online Dating Hope

S ome men distinguish themselves by being great scientists, statesmen, artists. I was a woman's last online dating hope. I did not choose or go after this "honor"—it was bestowed upon me by Emily, whom I met on an online dating site. Emily informed me that her experiences meeting online dates in person had been so horrible, so traumatic, so soul-draining, that she decided to give the process just one more chance. She'd decided to meet one more guy before removing herself from online dating for all eternity—and I happened to be the guy; the last guy she was going to meet; her final chance for online romance.

Of all the online dating sites, in all the towns, in all the world, she logs on to mine. After hanging up the phone, I found myself experiencing a range of emotions not unlike the Seven Stages of Grief. First, there was Cockiness—those other guys may have disappointed her, but I'll make up for them. Then,

Doubt—what if I don't measure up? Next, Resentment—what right does she have to place that "Last Man" burden upon me? Then, Guilt—if I turn out to be her final disappointment, it could push her over the edge; she could end up doing something drastic like taking her own life—or even worse, mine! Finally, Acceptance—ah, what am I worried about? It doesn't take much to see that the problems of two Jewish online daters don't amount to a hill of beans in this crazy world. I'll give it my best shot. That's all I can do. I owe the poor woman that much.

The fateful day arrived. As Emily's last online dating hope, I felt a sense of power. And yet with dating power comes great dating responsibility. I shaved, showered, and put on clean underwear—all things antithetical to basic male nature. I'd even carefully selected a little café with a funky, romantic atmosphere. As was my custom, I arrived early and asked the piano player to play one of my favorite romantic songs, James Brown's "Sex Machine." Sam didn't feel like playing it, but I was firm. "Play it." He started playing and, as if on cue, Emily walked in.

Or was it Emily's mother? She sort of looked like her photo—if her photo was taken twenty years earlier and thirty pounds lighter. The photo showed a young, happy woman with a short, trendy haircut. The in-person version was bigger, older, with long, shapeless hair, slumped shoulders, a beaten-down-by-life demeanor and personality, and some very odd facial expressions. Could her appearance have had something to do with Emily's negative dating experiences? Hey, what do I know? It's just a theory.

To say there was zero attraction is like saying the Ku Klux Klan has no Affirmative Action program. Every minute of that thirty-minute coffee date was an eternity. And those are thirty eternities I'll never get back again. The clincher—and my final nail-in-the-coffin test for any prospective romantic relationship—I asked her what she thought about the Beatles. She shrugged and said she could take them or leave them. I could never fully give myself to any woman who wasn't nuts about the Beatles. I wouldn't trust her.

At least I was honest. I told Emily I didn't feel any chemistry. And that I fully supported her idea of abandoning online dating. In fact, I told her in no uncertain terms, "If you don't get off that dating site, Emily, you'll regret it. Maybe not today, maybe not tomorrow, but soon and for the rest of your life." Her eyes misting, she touched my arm and said, "We'll always have Culver City." I gave her a final hug, and as I walked off into the fog, I remember thinking to myself, "Mark, this is *not* going to be the start of a beautiful friendship."

I wish I could have given Emily more wisdom and hope. Because shortly after meeting her, I did discover the very essence of the dating game.

Finding a Soul Mate Is a Numbers Game, Actually

OK, I'll admit it—I'm one of those romantics who believes that my soul mate is out there someplace. I just hope she's in the Los Angeles area, because if she's in Kentucky or Argentina, the dating commute is going to grow old pretty quickly, despite the obvious advantages to my frequent-flier mileage account.

Assuming as I do, though, that my soul mate is currently within the borders of California, my next concerns are:

1. How do I find her?
2. Will she also perceive me as her soul mate?
3. Will she (please, God) not be Lindsay Lohan?

Hey, you have your nightmares; I have mine.

Of course it would be so easy if, when you met your soul mate, he or she had a large neon sign overhead flashing "THIS

IS THE ONE!" But so few people are considerate enough to appear in our lives bearing the proper oversized neon identification. Hence, we must find other criteria.

These other criteria, at least for me, have included:

1. Chemistry.
2. Shared interests.
3. A meeting of minds.
4. Willingness to get naked with me.

OK, so No. 4 doesn't guarantee she's soul mate material, but it is indicative of the proper gung-ho attitude; it's a start.

I also worry about "settling." At what point do you look at the person across the table and say to yourself, *OK, I'm done looking. She has enough of what I want. I'll be with her.* And then not have the feeling a few months or years down the line, *Gee, her bright red hair, guttural German accent, and collection of antique soup ladles didn't seem quite so annoying when we first met.*

So when it comes to the qualities we want in a soul mate, how many of them are enough? If she has 75 percent of my desired attributes, should that be sufficient? Or would I feel that I'm settling and wonder if someone with 89 percent would have been just around the corner and much more satisfying? And if she was, would I truly be happy with her, when someone with 97 percent might have come along a month or two down the line?

Now do you understand my torment? And how important a working knowledge of arithmetic is in a single adult's daily life?

Clearly, no one person is going to have all the traits I'd ideally like my soul mate to possess. So, what am I willing to do without?

If she has great looks and a great job, can I do without her having a sense of humor? If she has a wonderful personality and laughs at everything I say, do I really mind that she looks a bit like my Uncle Arthur? And if she's nuts about me and is a sexual athlete, do I care that she moves her lips when she reads, and truly enjoys the thrills of monster truck rallies?

Everything in life seems to be less than perfect, a compromise. Our jobs are never quite ideal. Our meals are never up to par. Friends and family let us down. Books and movies disappoint. Even our bodies are not what we'd like. So why do we expect perfection in our romantic partners? We can't all be Brad Pitts and Jennifer Anistons. And even they surely have their flaws and problems. Yeah, right. Boo-hoo.

They say that with age comes wisdom. OK, so I've personally disproved that theory. But I have learned a thing or two. And one of the things I've learned is that when you're in a truly loving relationship, your partner's flaws are minimized and positive qualities maximized. Which is a really nice thing to happen, because it sends you deeper into love with them.

And when that happens, one day you look across the table and you don't think, *I wonder if I could have done better.* You think, *I am incredibly lucky to be with her.*

Then you touch her gently and tell her that her voice is like silk, her red hair has never looked lovelier and, in one final gesture of pure love, you offer to help her polish her soup ladles.

Of course, not everyone has acquired said wisdom about dating. Usually, I'm the one lacking it. But every now and then, I encounter this failing in a potential romantic partner.

The Sounds of Dating Silence

As far as I know, there are no such things as federal laws pertaining to dating etiquette. Oh, sure, there was that book *The Rules* several years back, but those weren't federal laws; those were simply man-made, or rather, woman-made rules or suggestions. As to why there are no federal laws governing dating etiquette—it's no doubt a matter of practicality. If there *were* actual laws governing dating behavior, no way would there be even one-eighth the necessary jail cells available to hold all the men who regularly violate said dating laws.

Of course, every now and then one encounters a dating law violator of the female persuasion. Which brings me to my recent date with Marina.

Admittedly, I would never have pegged Marina as the date lawbreaking type. Attractive, intelligent, sensitive, good sense of humor, and most importantly—seemed to really like me.

Our meeting on an online singles site led to very encouraging e-mailing, phoning, and finally, the all-important first meeting—lunch, my treat, where there seemed to be good chemistry, ending with her suggesting that I call her to set up date number two. So far, so good.

Of course, that was back in the good old days, before Marina and my relationship took several sudden and (at least on my part) unexpected turns toward The Dark Side. The afternoon following our lunch, I called Marina, reached her voice mail, and left a message thanking her for a lovely lunch, saying how much I enjoyed meeting her and that I was very much looking forward to our next date, which we can arrange when she calls me back.

I'm big on courtesy and appreciation, both giving it and receiving it, and was a bit disappointed that I hadn't already gotten a "thanks for the lunch/nice meeting you" e-mail from Marina. But I realize not everyone thinks like I do; otherwise the world would be even scarier. I'll probably get that thank-you when she calls me back, I reasoned.

As it turned out, it's a good thing I'm not a wait-by-the-phone-for-a-return-call kind of guy. Because Marina did not return my call that afternoon, evening, the following day, or even the day after that. Unless, God forbid, something terrible happened to her, thereby immobilizing her, it slowly dawned on me that *People* magazine would most likely not be reserving photo space for me and Marina in their Lovers of the Year issue.

Any reasonable man in this situation would have simply gotten the silent message loud and clear, written Marina off, and moved on to greener, more appreciative pastures. But this is me we're talking about. I felt the need to let Marina know that although I got the message (or lack thereof) that she was not interested in meeting again, I felt it was discourteous on her part to a) not e-mail a "thank you for lunch, it was nice meeting you, but I didn't feel the magic, good luck" kind of acknowledgment, and b) to have ignored my call after she invited me to call.

This finally motivated Marina to respond, and I quote: "While it is obvious you know nothing about me, your missive revealed so much about you. You are a pompous, pathetic man. Grow up." Okay, that did it. I immediately crossed Marina's name off my Hanukkah card list.

But in truth, I was baffled. Perhaps I delude myself in thinking that most people, and especially women, have a certain degree of humanity, sensitivity, and consideration. And perhaps this is payback, with Marina having reversed the traditional male-female roles, with her taking on the male role of the love 'em and leave 'em cad, and me becoming the female who needs to communicate feelings.

I'd rather, though, think of it this way—most people I meet are sensitive, appreciative, and caring. So when I encounter one who does not have those qualities, it only serves to make me appreciate the others all the more. Of course, when I become King of the Universe, dating laws will require thank-yous and immediate, considerate responses. Too bad, Marina. You could have been my queen.

At this point, it seemed as though I was on a breakups roll.

Death of a Relationship

OK, I'll admit it—I've made every possible mistake in the world of romantic relationships. But do I accept full responsibility? Of course not. I blame it on school, where they teach you geometry, philosophy, biology, ancient history, French, art—yes, every conceivable subject except how to have a successful romantic relationship. That subject you have to figure out all for yourself. And I'm a slow learner. So I estimate that women will really be impressed with my relationship skills by the time I'm ninety.

Considering the fact that my coming of age as a romantic partner is still decades ahead of me, perhaps I shouldn't have been as stunned as I was when Abby chose to end the seven-month relationship I thought was going so well. Still, this breakup caught me by surprise.

For one thing, you don't expect a breakup to occur during a romantic vacation in Santa Barbara. One that involved a train trip and a luncheon at a restaurant on the pier and a tandem bike ride along the boardwalk and a stroll through an art museum. But apparently, this happened to be Cupid's weekend off. And when Cupid's off duty, anything that can go wrong romantically, does.

After the long train ride, for example, we both collapsed on the motel bed and started to kiss. Shortly thereafter, as required by the Male Rules of International Make-Out Law, I began to unbutton her blouse. Suddenly, the temperature in the room dropped forty degrees. Abby was upset that the curtain was open and anyone who walked by our poolside room outside could look in and see us. OK, so I'll close the curtains. But why be upset about it? It seemed so at odds with Abby's normal demeanor and delight in being with me, that I was too thrown off base to pursue it verbally.

What followed that day, however, was a series of "Nothing You Do Is Right" experiences. Apparently, though I thought the relationship was going well 'til now, Abby had been busy accumulating a list of dissatisfactions and chose this vacation day to dump them on me. Abby's grievances:

- I stopped on our bike ride to speak with a lifeguard about what he'd recommend we check out in the area. This was symptomatic of my chatting with other people during our dates, which takes away from quality alone time as a couple.

- I watched our bike as she took a shell-gathering walk on the beach since bikes weren't allowed on the beach. When she came back, she found me on the cell phone, wishing my daughter good luck at summer camp for the next morning. Abby said, "I knew you couldn't just be here enjoying the beach; you'd have to be on the phone. You can't be alone with your thoughts."

- I started telling Abby about my brief talk, while she was shell-gathering, with a couple preparing for their wedding on the beach. Abby said she wasn't interested, and why did I always have to, again, take the focus away from our relationship by talking to others, and strangers at that?

- On a part of the train ride up to Santa Barbara, I was talking "shop" (writer talk) with the person seated across from us (who, by the way, was the whole reason we were taking this trip since I'd won the trip by submitting an entry to his radio show). But, again, not focusing entirely on Abby.

- I repeat phrases. For example, during the ride to the motel, someone was describing a delicious meal they had, and I said, "The only problem with that kind of meal is what are you going to look forward to when you get to heaven?" Abby mentioned that as an example of phrases I repeat, and it gets on her nerves.

Well, you get the idea. What followed was a whole lot of uncomfortable silence, some tears, and the end of the relationship. I acknowledge my shortcomings. I acknowledge that Abby had some issues that may not have had anything to do with me. Still, it's scary that a relationship you think is going really well can come to a grinding halt so rapidly. It's scary how much you have to learn about relationships, no matter how old or experienced you are. And it's especially scary that, no matter how much you learn from your relationship mistakes, there is always a world of new mistakes to make. (Sigh.)

One of the scariest things about the ending of a romantic relationship for me is its velocity—how very quickly it can come to a grinding halt. Of course, if a relationship has to end, there's an art to ending it as well.

When the Music's Over

The end of a romantic relationship is like a little death. And some people just don't do death well. After ten extremely passionate months together, Melissa decided to end our relationship. She thought it through very carefully and took the steps she felt were necessary to break things off. There was just one small step she overlooked—telling me.

So here's how I found out. Coming home after work one night, I noticed that the clothing Melissa usually kept hanging in my closet was gone—just the empty hangers in their place. The stuff she kept in the bathroom—also gone. I was expecting her that night, and she never appeared. My phone message to her was not returned. No word from her for the next two days. Had she been kidnapped? Been in an accident? Spoken to one of my old girlfriends about me? I called her sister and left a message, but never heard back from her, either.

Finally, after two days, there was a message from Melissa on my phone machine: "I'm out of town for a few days. I needed to get away to think about our relationship." Which, as it happened to turn out, is woman-speak for "You'll see me naked again when the Pope becomes a rabbi." I finally reached her by phone. What followed was a half-hour conversation, in which Melissa told me she was leaving because, basically, she wanted a different kind of guy.

"But you seemed so happy with the guy you had during our ten extremely passionate months together," I reminded her. And I pointed out things she had said to me frequently, little things like "I love you," "You're the man I've been waiting for all my life," and "This is the most incredible relationship I've ever had." None of that mattered now. Her mind was made up, her heart was closed down, the security systems were activated, and that was the last time we communicated.

As psychiatrists are fond of saying, "and how did that make you feel?" Well, I felt shocked, depressed, angry, abused, mislead, hurt, and abandoned—which, incidentally, were the actual names of the Seven Dwarves before Disney started fiddling with them. But then I got to wondering why Melissa chose to dump me in such a cold fashion when what preceded it was ten months of passion. And the only thing I could come up with was that Melissa chose to take the easy way out—for her. She didn't want a confrontation, an argument, or the pain of raw, exposed emotion, so she simply left. And left me holding the big, unopened Pandora's box of sudden loss.

But painful experiences are invariably learning experiences, and what I learned from Melissa's emotional cowardice is that there is an art, if you will, to breaking off a relationship. That is assuming, of course, that your intention is to behave like a human being, to honor the relationship, and to be considerate and respectful of your partner's feelings. Think of it as a farewell gift to your partner. Or think of it simply as the right thing to do.

For the love of God, don't just suddenly vanish. Nor should you do it via phone, e-mail, letter, or through a third party's intervention. All of those techniques are simply wimping out, hurtful, and just plain wrong. You know it, I know it, Dr. Phil knows it.

The only way to end a relationship is face to face. Raise the issues. See if there's a chance to work them out or get help to do so. If not, tell him or her the honest reasons. And also acknowledge all the good in the relationship. If you sense there's a mutual desire to stay friends, discuss that. If not, wish your partner happiness and good luck, give him or her a hug, and leave.

Remember how kind and gentle, thoughtful, and respectful you were going into the relationship? Well, your exit strategy should involve those identical qualities. But be forewarned—if you don't use those qualities, I sincerely hope that the giant, angry Karma Monster tracks you down and torments you in the Extreme Punishment Room for all eternity. Oh, and by the way, if you see Melissa there, give her my regards, won't you?

But in the meantime, check this out: I finally encounter a new, revised, kind of unexpected and updated fairy-tale ending to my romantic history.

The Less I See You, The More I Love You

Sometimes I think about my former marriage. After years of no dates, bad dates, or simply wham-bam-thank-you-ma'am dates, I'd met someone who had life partner/first-marriage potential, someone who could be my first real adult relationship. I held on tighter than Donald Trump to a bad hairstyle. I love you, I say. I want to be with you all the time, I say. Let's get married, I say. I say a lot of things. We get married. At first, it's just like in the movies. There's love and sex and caring and sharing and laughter and plans for the future. We could be modeling for Hallmark greeting cards.

There are fields of daisies and we're running across them, in slow motion, toward one another, with arms outstretched. It couldn't be mushier, cornier, or gayer, but we don't give a damn. Other singles are envying us. "Be strong, little singles," we tell them. "We were you once."

Flash forward. A few years. A couple of kids. A few conflicts. "I want you" has been replaced by "Are you still here?" "Do you realize we've been having sex for six straight hours?" has been replaced by "Do you realize we haven't had sex for six straight weeks?" And "I just love all your little quirks" has been replaced by "That sound you make when you sneeze makes my skin crawl." Being together day after day sadly has lost its luster.

What in the world is happening to the arc of my romantic growth? I seem to have gone from "All You Need Is Love" to "Familiarity Breeds Contempt" to "Absence Makes the Heart Grow Fonder."

What kind of romantic flowchart is that for a supposedly evolving single adult male's love life? And I do consider myself a romantic. This was reinforced by all the love songs, movies, TV commercials, and my parents' loving relationship to which I was exposed, not to mention the many dry spells wishing I had a loving relationship. Of course, when you're alone, you look around and it appears as though everyone else in the world is in love except you. All the other animals on the Ark are in pairs—except you, the sole pig—Porky, party of one.

We tried to save the quickly expiring marital patient. Counseling. More counseling. More counseling. But it was not to be. We decide to pull the plug. Divorce. Mediation. Married couple becomes two single Porkies again.

Jump back into the quest. Dating. Periods of no dates, bad dates, wham-bam-thank-you-ma'am dates. And once again, finally, after a long dry spell, I meet someone who has life partner potential. Wait a minute. This is starting to sound familiar. I try to remember the TV show or movie that's reminding me of what's happening—until it occurs to me that it's a rerun from my own life. Oh, God. I'm repeating the pattern.

Will I be stuck in this Dante's Romantic Inferno forever? Will this be my personal hell? My Vietnam? My Iraq?

Because of our work, children, pet, and activity schedules, this new girlfriend and I can only see each other a few times a week. But each time we do, it's like we're meeting for that first time. We're constantly in a state of missing each other and accumulating experiences and feelings to share. We're not together every day. We're definitely not living together. And we're both fine with that. Really. We've each been married before, so neither of us are in a hurry to rush into anything permanent. We each value both our time together and our independent time apart.

I remember many of those fairy tales we read as kids ending with: "And they lived together, happily ever after." I suppose for some people that still holds true. But for myself and for many others these days, it's a new, revised fairy tale ending: "And they lived *apart*, happily ever after." Maybe it's not the perfect fairy tale ending. Then again, what with the national divorce rate at 50 percent and higher, maybe we're simply creating our own fairy tale.

And as I was to find out, even dating fairy tales have their own dating laws, with violators of those laws on both sides of the dating gender spectrum.

SECTION TWO:
MY OBSERVATIONS
ON DATING AND ROMANCE

Sometimes I enjoy ruminating about the art and science of dating and romance—without tying those thoughts into specific dates I've had, as in Section One, above. That's what follows in this next section. I hope you enjoy it as much as I enjoyed using the word "ruminating."

Whatever Happened to Woo?

I wish I lived 200 years ago so I could woo a woman the way single men did back then. Who even uses the word "woo" anymore, much less knows what it means? Who even gives much thought at all to what they say to the opposite sex? Maybe Kanye West, but the rest of us— not so much.

The media and the MTV generation and life's increasingly rapid pace have pretty much finished off traditional courtship, replacing "wooing" with "hitting on" or "coming on to" or "making your move." It's so sad. Where's the poetry? Where's the passion? Where's the heart? For many of us men, unfortunately, it's all in our pants. OK, I'll speak for myself.

But, back then, a single man's brains were located substantially higher up. A single man put some thought into his pursuit of romance. It mattered to him, and he showed it. The dude could woo. He was one lean, mean, wooing machine.

Take this excerpt of a letter from French novelist Victor Hugo to his beloved Adele, on one Friday evening, March 15, 1822:

"My Adele, my adorable and adored Adele. . . . I have been asking myself every moment if such happiness is not a dream. It seems to me that what I feel is not of earth. I cannot yet comprehend this cloudless heaven. . . . Oh, Adele, do not mistake these words for blind enthusiasm—enthusiasm for you has lasted all my life, and increased day by day. My whole soul is yours. . . . Soon—in a few months, perhaps, my angel will sleep in my arms, will awaken in my arms, will live there. All your thoughts at all moments, all your looks will be for me; all my thoughts, all my moments, all my looks, will be for you! My Adele! Adieu; pardon the delirium of one who embraces you, and who adores you, both for this life and another."

My God—that's foreplay on paper! But sadly, such romantic language appears today less frequently than a Jean Claude Van Damme movie on the Lifetime channel. Don't believe me? Check out some online dating profiles. Go on; I'll wait . . . Let me guess—you found maybe one or two that were well written, sophisticated, charming, romantic, and enticing. But many profiles on online dating sites, sadly, are a repository of stock phrases, trite expressions, tired metaphors, and colorless language. It's a case of the bland leading the bland.

This is a shame because an online dating profile could (and should) be an opportunity to showcase one's romantic soul, to add poetry, beauty, and wonder to the quest for a soul mate, to demonstrate one's ability to worship and adore a potential life partner through literary caresses. And, yet, what do I see on every third woman's profile I view? Dribble. The same dribble: "I'm as comfortable in a cocktail dress as I am in jeans."

Let me repeat that, since it represents one of the most overused and lame phrases appearing in these profiles and is thus worthy of our studied scorn: "I'm as comfortable in a cocktail dress as I am in jeans."

Will someone explain to me what the hell that means? Could it mean that I won't have to worry about her cocktail dress causing her to break out in hives and scratch herself bloody? That I can take her to Subway in her cocktail dress for the turkey meal deal? That I shouldn't be surprised if she meets me for a game of beach volleyball in her cocktail dress?

Tell me, is this a female trait guys desire? It must be because so many women mention it. I mean, I have a number of single male friends, and I honestly can't recall the last time any of them said to me, "Y'know, Amy is a wonderful woman, but I just don't think it'll work—she's nowhere near as comfortable in her cocktail dress as she is in jeans."

But I digress. The point is the steady erosion of the language of love. And I think modern romance is suffering as a result. Now, I realize we men can't just, all of the sudden, up and start making love-talk like Hugo. As lovely as it is, women would perceive it as corny, old-fashioned, and metrosexual.

Still, perhaps we can sneak a little of it in here and there. And that, combined with deleting all references to our comfort in formal wear, our love of taking long walks on the beach, and our realization that you shouldn't go to bed angry and that you can't change anyone—might just add up to one small step toward keeping it real, original, and romantic. Now, if you'll excuse me, I have to go put on my tux and go bowling. Don't worry; I'll be just as comfortable.

Of course, we men can woo all we want, but there remains a plethora of other mistakes we can and do make in the world of romance.

Mistakes Men Make in Romance

O K, I'll admit it—we men excel at messing up our romantic lives. This is why romantic songs and movies and Hallmark cards are so popular—among women. They bring women a world of Enrique and Antonio and Romeo, instead of the world of women's unshaven, unemployed date asleep on the couch, in his underwear, snoring, drool dangling from his lips, a half-eaten bag of Cheetos spilled out onto the floor he's never vacuumed. Of course, that's generally the photo men fail to post on their online dating profile.

On dates, women like to be taken to fine restaurants and sophisticated evenings of theater, or perhaps a British romantic film, followed by some insightful conversation, and then directly home, with perhaps some casual, witty flirting at the door, before saying good night.

A man's fantasy date? A triple Wham-Bam Burger at Hooters restaurant, the latest superhero movie, and then having at each other like wild monkeys at the Sin-Sational Motor Lodge, featuring heated, revolving water beds, complimentary Day-Glo love gels, and overhead mirrors. Or so I've heard.

Men use cologne when they start dating. This gives women the mistaken impression that their man naturally smells like an exotic rain forest or tropical island breeze, and will always smell that way. Is it any wonder, then, that problems arise later, when the man feels he's got the woman and no longer needs the cologne? For now his natural aroma is a mixture of beer, tobacco, three-day-old underwear, the dog, last night's pork 'n' garlic burrito, really funky sweat, and something that died an agonizing death months ago.

Once sex has occurred, women expect their dates to cuddle. Cuddling and talking is bearable for maybe the first minute and a half afterwards. Beyond that, centuries of male genetics kick in, so that even while the woman may be talking about her feelings that you are different from any other man she's ever known, the man's brain is filled only with images of having a pepperoni pizza while watching something sexy on pay-per-view—something with absolutely no cuddling and talking after sex. In fact, the end of each scene just cuts to another scene of a different couple having sex and not cuddling or talking afterwards.

Men believe that God wouldn't have given them the ability to make gross noises with their various body parts if He didn't want them to do so. OK, let's, just for the sake of argument, say this is true. Nonetheless, it nauseates women. Yes, even if you say "Excuse me" afterwards. Or swear the dog did it. Women never believe that, and the dog ends up resenting you.

Women feel they don't have to inform their men why they're upset; men should just know. The odds are really against this one working, simply because men make so many mistakes all day long, that to have to guess which of them is ticking their woman off would be not only time-consuming, but plain lucky.

Should the date evolve into a marriage, men expect women to earn a living, take care of the house, raise the kids, and be eager for sex every night. And what do men do in return? Once every three weeks, they're asked to open the lid of a jar. After doing so, they get this look on their faces, as if to say, "What would you do without me, babe?"

Finally, women expect men to say, "I love you." This one is not a mistake. Women need to hear it. And men need to say it a lot more often—even if it means shouting it from the other room while they are finishing their pizza. Hey, it's the thought.

Bottom line—men's and women's brains work differently. And while I can't pretend to speak to men with authority about how women's brains work, I can speak to women from personal experience about the mysteries of the male brain.

A Woman's Guide to the Inner Workings of A Man's Brain

The hip, cutting-edge magicians Penn & Teller are often resented and discredited by more traditional magicians because the bad boys of magic invariably give away the secrets of how their tricks are done as part of their show. They commit what the other magicians see as the cardinal sin: revealing the sham behind the illusion.

In order to educate the fairer sex, I am about to embark upon a similar endeavor, at the risk of incurring the wrath of my entire gender. My agenda is to reveal to women vital information about men, which up until this moment was understood only by Dr. Phil and the woman who answers the phone when you call 1-900-HOTCHAT—to reveal the sham behind the male illusion.

What follows, then, is a woman's guide to the inner workings of a man's brain. Read it and weep. And, just a short note to my male readers—please don't hate me because I am honest.

Cerebrum – Cerebral hemispheres control speech, memory, and intelligence. Although it's the largest component of the brain, whenever a man approaches a beautiful woman, it invariably shrinks to the size of a sesame seed. If he gets shot down, the cerebrum releases a defense mechanism enzyme which convinces the man he's better off without her, as she is undoubtedly a lesbian.

Cerebellum – Responsible for coordinating movement and maintaining balance. Used primarily when a man has had eight beers and is endeavoring to make his way to the bathroom without tripping over the dog and pulling the fish tank over on top of them.

Hypothalamus – Influences sleep, appetite, and sexual desire. This is the brain part most valued by men. It is used most fully on Saturday nights, when men have sex, scarf down some pizza, and then drop off in bed, dead to the world.

Cartoid and vertebral arteries – They feed the brain and its components with oxygen and nutrients. These brain parts are optional for Motor Vehicle Department clerks, television programming executives, and men whose given name is Bubba.

Occipital lobe – Receives and analyzes visual information. Example: *"Ooh, check out that state-of-the-art sports car, which costs three times my yearly salary. I think I can swing it if I cut back on food, rent, and medical insurance. I hope that it's available in red."*

Temporal lobe – Deals with sound. Responsible for convincing man singing in shower that he is smoother than Enrique Iglesias.

Also automatically drops voice three octaves when he is introduced to a woman he finds attractive.

Medulla – Controls breathing and the heartbeat, both of which stop during the viewing of any televised sporting event.

Cranial nerves – Control eye and tongue movements. Used primarily at the beach, in response to noticing any woman in a thong bikini within a five-mile radius. Pupils become dilated; involuntary drooling occurs. Often accompanied by a swat on the head from one's date, together with the man's exclamation, *"What woman?!"*

Corpus callosum – A massive bundle of nerve tracts connecting the brain's two hemispheres. In one out of fifty men, these nerve tracts are nonexistent resulting in the impulse to purchase lifetime subscriptions to *Penthouse* magazine and, while cruising in one's car and spotting any woman under seventy, rolling down one's window and making tiny sucking sounds at her in an attempt to prove one's value as a suitor.

All right, ladies, now that you're experts on the male brain, are you ready to jump back into the dating world? Before doing so, please allow me to make a pitch for something else about which I can speak from plenty of personal experience—the benefits of Internet dating.

How Internet Dating Beats the Pants Off Off-Line Dating!

I know you're not gonna believe this, but before Internet dating sites, couples actually used to meet "off-line"— out in public, often by chance, at parties, dances, supermarkets, museums, bookstores. No, really! But like the Tyrannosaurus rex, the Edsel automobile, and Steven Segal's career, off-line dating is seemingly on its way to extinction. Oh, sure, a few couples occasionally meet off-line, as God intended, in the course of their daily lives, much like our pioneer ancestors, but they're just lucky and we resent them. Just because they didn't have to pay $25 a month, post a photo, write a profile, and proceed to meet hundreds of people with whom they felt less chemistry than Dick Cheney and Barbra Streisand on a Tunnel of Love ride—must they rub their joy in our faces?

More and more singles are meeting via Internet dating sites. There's gotta be a reason for that. In fact, there are exactly four reasons why Internet dating beats the pants off of off-line dating. (And please forgive me for that image—I blame it on a literary wardrobe malfunction).

1. **Comfort Level** – You can check out prospective dates from the comfort of your home, wearing nothing but your bunny slippers and "Just Do Me!" boxer shorts. Okay, I'll speak for myself. But how great is it that you don't have to shave, shower, get dressed, drive someplace, be hit on by people in whom you have no interest, and then drive home, feeling that you've spent a large chunk of time with no noticeable results? It's enough to make a guy swear off dating completely and decide to simply date himself. And, yes, that is weird, but I've found I have an amazing amount of things in common with myself, and, not to get too personal, but—I'm always in the mood.

2. **Information Level** – Knowledge is power, and when you date online, you have access to substantial information about your prospective dates before you even contact them. It might take you two weeks to work up the courage to ask out that supermarket cashier, only to find out that she's a) married, b) gay, or c) a smoker who's just invited her mother to move into her place to help care for her four hyperactive kids. Whereas with online dating, much is revealed through the person's profile, photos, the initial phone call, hiring that detective to do a background check, and searching for every mention of their name on Google or local bathroom stalls.

3. **Security Level** – Once, at a yard sale, I was hit on by a woman who was clearly attempting to turn on the charm.

I don't blame her. She had no way of knowing that her combination of Attention Deficit Disorder, skin surface resembling a topographic map of the Appalachian Mountain chain, and a dog that barfed on my sneakers is generally not my cup of tea. My point here is that with online dating, you choose whom you want to pursue romantically. Not that you don't make mistakes. Not that people don't misrepresent themselves. But at least you don't have that queasy feeling of having to deal, at any moment, with a surprise visit from Typhoid Mary, or her sister, Restraining Order Rhonda.

4. **Quantity Level** – We all know that meeting one's soul mate is a numbers game. You've got to kiss a lot of frogs before you meet your prince or princess. And by then, you've got hundreds of profiles of romantic candidates in one evening, if you so choose. Contact ten of them, not hear back from four, talk to six on the phone, rule out three, meet three for coffee, like one but she doesn't like you, are liked by one but you don't like her, and the one you agree to meet for a second date informs you a few days later that she's decided to get back together with her last boyfriend. Just try accomplishing all that with off-line dating!

Do I have any advice for men before they jump into the dating world? Did you even have to ask?

Whether it's online or off-line dating, one thing is clear: just one of the two genders is in command. Can you guess which one?

It's a Woman's World—
We Men Only Date in It

In the wonderful wide world of dating, there are those (primarily women) who feel that men have it easy and women get the short end of the stick. Then there are those (primarily men) who feel that romance is a woman's world and it's men who continually get *el shafto grando* (OK, so Spanish wasn't my best subject in school).

Finally, there are those who say, "Hey, what with world famine, war, disease, and the depletion of the ozone layer, don't you people have something more meaningful with which to occupy yourselves than arguing over who has it easier in dating? What's wrong with you? You sicken us!" But those most likely are people who are jealous of our active dating lives. They probably couldn't get a date if they tripped over one at a singles party. We feel sorry for them. Let's just ignore them. And let's focus on the dating world for women. Because we're gentlemen. We like to be polite to women and do nice things for them to butter them up so that they'll have sex with us later. Oops, I wasn't supposed to mention that; it was supposed to be a secret. Well, cat's out of the bag now.

But it doesn't take an Einstein to realize that women hold the keys to the romance kingdom—and right from the start. 99 percent of the time, it's we guys who must make the first move and ask the women out. The burden for being proactive falls on us. We must determine the right words to say, the right time to say them, and the right way to say them. And we bear all the risk of failure. All the woman needs to do is say yes or no. Boo-hoo, how very challenging for her. We're the ones who must crawl back to our corner, beaten and rejected, licking our wounds.

Once the dating has gone on for a while, women are the only one of the genders who knows whether the date will end in hot, sweaty, pulsating monkey love—or as the Canadians refer to it, sex. Men hope it will, they boast to their buddies it will, they use all their powers of persuasion on the woman to convince her it will—but in the end, it's the woman's decision. Now, that's power. And that's easier for her.

Shall we talk economics? The flowers, restaurant, movie tickets, gifts, parking. I can sum it up in three words: the guy pays. Oh, sure, there are women who pay. I believe there are approximately eleven of them in the known universe. They make way more money than their dates. They have better jobs than their dates. They have better homes than their dates. In general, though, men are the ones who open their wallets. They take the financial hit. Is that fair? No. Is that expected? Yes. Will women think less of men and share tales of their men's cheapness with their girlfriends if men fail to open their wallets? You bet. Advantage—women.

And don't even get me started on birth control. Is there even one form of it used by women that approaches the awkwardness, discomfort, and sensation-smothering nature of the condom? At least women get their birth control material by prescription, via the relative privacy of the pharmacist. Condoms are all over-the-counter, causing every customer in line plus the checkout clerk and bag boy to know what I'll be doing that weekend, if I need the maxi-size, if I prefer "ribbed for her comfort," and if I like them in colors. It's a woman's world when it comes to birth control.

How about just walking around together on the date? Could that possibly have been constructed to favor the woman and make her life easier? Indeed. Especially if you're both excited to be with one another. Woman excited—no visual difference. Man excited—Mount Rushmore attempting to escape his pants. Embarrassment. People pointing. Young children asking, "Mommy, what's that? I'm scared!" And when the clothing comes off, women can play it cool, not letting on how turned on they are. Not men. With us, it's a big red flag—or, rather, flagpole. Granted, it may not be the military, but we're saluting women constantly, whether we consciously want it to happen or not.

The whole Victorian mindset about women being delicate flowers who should be protected from exerting any physical effort seems to be continuing into the 21st century. Women on dates need never even touch a door. A man opens a woman's car door, restaurant door, and nightclub door for her. Why? If you find out, please let me know. Perhaps it should be the other way around, with the woman opening doors for the man. After all, his arms are so weak from constantly reaching into his wallet for her, he'd no doubt appreciate that consideration. But, no.

In fact, men, how often does your date take advantage of her "delicate" nature vs. your "great big manly strength," requesting that you change her lightbulb, take out her garbage, get a heavy box down from the attic, lift the back end of her car up so she can free the bicycle messenger she just ran over? And we do it all, unquestioningly and uncomplainingly. Why? Because our penis is completely under her spell, sending us thought commands to "Obey the woman and she'll make it worth your while . . . obey . . . obey . . . " Yes, master.

OK, I think we've established by now that women have it way easier when it comes to dating. As a matter of fact, they also have it easier in the working world, they generally outlive men, they can charm their way out of traffic tickets, and they're constantly being offered seats on the bus, free perfume samples in department stores, and free admission to various nightclubs. No wonder so many men have sex-change operations. They want in on the good life.

Another key to the good life: pairing up things that can benefit you romantically. Allow me to explain.

Thanksgivukkah: Not the Only Pairing That Can Benefit You Romantically

n 2013, Thanksgiving and Hanukkah fell on the same day, and folks referred to it as Thanksgivukkah. Catchy, huh? And just check out a few of the benefits associated with this rare, two-in-one holiday:

- Two agonizing holiday meals with relatives were magically transformed into one agonizing meal.
- It's a golden opportunity to experience firsthand what you'd always suspected: how well turkey goes with latkes.
- The Macy's Thanksgiving Day Parade finally featured a giant dreidel float surrounded by dancing rabbis.
- It's proof Thanksgiving is more fun with presents and gelt!
- The president could pardon both the Thanksgiving turkey and the Hanukkah blintz.

The pairing of Thanksgiving and Hanukkah as Thanks-givukkah works so well, it raises the question among us daters—why not pair up even more things in your life that can benefit you romantically? Here are some suggestions.

1. Chocsters

We all know oysters are legendary for having aphrodisiac qualities. As is chocolate. Combining them will no doubt double their romantic potency. I propose oyster-flavored chocolate bars to be marketed as Chocsters. Admit it, guys, how much fun would it be to whisper into your date's ear, "Hey, baby, want to come back to my place to try my oyster-flavored chocolate bar?" No doubt that's not an offer she gets every day!

2. Fluquila

Most people hate getting shots. Half the folks I know avoid flu shots because the shots just haven't been marketed well. It's all in the presentation. Make the flu shot pleasant to receive, tasty, and with an appealing aftereffect. Picture the flu shots in a liquid format, mixed with tequila—your choice of flavors. The result? A health item that also lowers one's romantic inhibitions. People would be lined up around the block at the doctor's office just waiting for "Flu Shot Happy Hour" to begin. Under the drinking age? No problem. Flugum—flu shots in bubble gum form. Hey, how do I make the Nobel Prize Committee aware of my suggestions?

3. Valenween Day

What could make more sense than taking two great holidays, Valentine's Day and Halloween, and combining them into one superholiday—Valenween Day? Sorry, kids, this one's for us adults only. Costumes include history's greatest lovers: Romeo and Juliet, Casanova, Bill Clinton, Anthony Weiner. "Tricks" take on a whole new meaning in trick or treating, as do "treats," for that matter. The only frightening part of the holiday is when your romantic partner is just not in the mood.

4. Jobation

Combine your job with your vacation to get this entirely new, state-of-the-art hybrid, a jobation. First, you can toss out that stodgy office chair. It will be replaced with your own, personal-sized Jacuzzi from which you'll do all your work. The office will be decorated in a tropical theme, with an actual beach recreated for your morning and afternoon breaks. Employees who do well will be rewarded with luaus, tropical drinks, and hula lessons. And you'll never want to go home because each night features gambling fun and a Vegas-style show. This ain't your father's job. Just *try* avoiding office romance with all this going on!

5. Taxssage

Nobody likes doing their taxes. Everyone loves getting a massage. It doesn't take a genius to realize that combining the two is a win-win situation: get your taxes done and get your relaxation done at the same time! How does it work? I was hoping you'd ask. Simply show up at one of the chain offices of "H&R Un-Block Your Tense Muscles." Bring your receipts. Request your choice of male or female, Swedish or shiatsu income or corporate. And if it turns out you need an extension, that's the perfect reason for a return visit. You're sure to find out what accountants have known for centuries—there's romance in numbers.

6. Sportswashing

Most men look at the prospect of washing the dishes in much the same way that most women look at the prospect of attending a Three Stooges Film Festival—number 867 on their priority list, just after snaking the bathroom drain. And yet to most men, watching sports games is like catnip. The solution? Turn the entire kitchen sink wall into a TV sports screen. Oh, sure, there's a bit of expense up front. But consider the advantages: The men do the dishes every night, the women are free to relax and are so grateful that they later show their appreciation in a very special way, if you catch my drift. Sportswashing—a sure step to ramping up the romance in your life. You're welcome.

Now, you try combining some things in your life for your romantic benefit and let me know what happens. Come on; I ask so little of you. And if you do it right, who knows? You could soon find yourself competing for the gold in the Dating Decathalon.

Going for the Dating Gold

Consider the Summer Olympics. The world's best athletes go for the gold. I've pretty much accepted the fact that my window of opportunity to become an Olympic athlete has closed. Although my window of opportunity is still way open to get one of those plush lounge chairs with the minifridge built into the side so I don't have to get up and walk all the way to the kitchen to get a beer.

But we singles in Los Angeles aim for another kind of gold—the dating gold—a relationship that works. And who's to say that our preparation for the dating gold is any less grueling than that of our athletic counterparts? OK, pretty much everybody. Still, we don't need steroids or international ceremonies or cereal box endorsements. Though we wouldn't turn the cereal box endorsement down. We just want chemistry with the right person. And not to have to take that long walk back across the dance floor to our grinning buddies who just witnessed a woman saying "no thanks" after we asked her to dance. And not to have to start over on Match.com every three weeks.

The really hard part begins after finding the relationship—making the relationship last. Because to make a relationship last, you have to be really effective in the relationship. And to be really effective in a relationship, you need the dating precision of an athlete—a dating athlete. No, make that a decathlete, for you need multiple skills. You've got to master the Dating Decathlon. That's ten dating events. Master these, and you can wear the bronze, silver, and gold dating medals with pride:

- **Equestrian Jumping Over Relationship Baggage**, which includes previous girlfriends and boyfriends, resentful family members, broken hearts, shattered dreams, and a "Maria & Vinnie Forever" tattoo acquired just before Vinnie began serving seven to ten for armed robbery.

- **Sailing the Sea of Love.** Stay downwind from your date after having the triple-garlic burrito. Don't get upset if she laughs at your dinghy. And if it looks like the relationship's going to sink, bail!

- **Greco-Roman Wrestling For the Check.** This is recognized as the world's oldest competitive sport. It's also the world's least surprising sport because the man always wins. If he lets the woman get the check, he can pretty much forget about any half nelson, or any other kind of nelson, that night.

- **Relationship Aquatics** includes Diving for Your Dignity after judgment is passed on your apartment, car, friends, job, and clothing; Synchronized Kissing to make sure you both want to do it at the same time, and Perfume Polo, which involves selecting a scent that won't make your date heave.

- **Dating Basketball** deals primarily with the courting that occurs off the court. You've got to master the assist, avoid personal fouls, and when having a serious discussion about your relationship, if you have any hope of making that slam dunk, for the love of God, do not dribble!

OK, I've gotten you started with five of the ten Dating Decathlon events. I'm sure you don't expect me to do all your relationship work for you. You'll figure the others out. And if not, there's always the *Winter* Dating Olympics—and you've already got a head start there: Most of us who've had relationships are well experienced skating on thin ice.

As if all that weren't overwhelming enough, I'll throw in this extra gift for women, and at no extra charge—something that will make communicating with men much more understandable.

Male-to-Female Dating Dictionary

Much of the reason dates often turn out so disastrously, especially first dates, is, in a word, communication. Yes, communication—or, as we men refer to it, Kryptonite. I'll admit it—men stink at it. We either can't or won't communicate. And when we do, we invariably do it poorly.

Reasons? Take your pick:

- Men are raised to be stoic and not reveal our true feelings and emotions.
- We fear that being honest and open will be perceived as a sign of weakness.
- In school, they never taught us how to communicate with another human being.

- Our primary communicating experience is talking and/or bragging to other guys about sports and women.
- Space aliens have zapped that portion of our brain required for being real.

So, because we're so lousy at relating to females, we invariably torpedo a relationship before it even has a fighting chance. Sad, isn't it? And all we have to make up for it and console ourselves are big cars, weight lifting, Häagen-Dazs, serial dating, the Playboy channel, and starting wars in third world nations. Yes, it's a pathetic, tragic, empty life, simply because we lack the skills of being open, honest, and vulnerable with, for want of a better word, women.

But, as you know, another outstanding feature of men, besides our inability to communicate, is our urge to—and feeling that we can and must—fix everything.

Therefore, I decided to take a portion of all the free time I have as a result of not using it to communicate openly and honestly with females—and put it to work coming up with a fix for this pesky communications problem. And lo and behold, I've found it! And it's beautiful in its simplicity, if I do say so myself. I call it, simply, the "Male-to-Female Dating Dictionary." This is a book of words and phrases uttered by dating males, translated into language clearly understandable to dating females. What a guy says—translated into what a guy means. I'll pause briefly here while a choir of dating angels sing hosannas to my public service accomplishment. OK, that's enough.

This is a book, obviously, that every dating woman needs, for it will instantly translate Martian men's conversation into Venutian women-speak. For example, from the beginner's level:

MAN SAYS: "Oh, um, sure, I like to dance."

MAN MEANS: "I once gave myself a hernia in a swing dance class, and now, on my list of things I enjoy, dancing comes right after cleaning up after a large dog with severe digestive problems.

MAN SAYS: "What I really want is a long-term, serious relationship with someone."

MAN MEANS: "And you could be that person if you consider *long-term* to be three months, and *serious* to include vodka, a wardrobe from Victoria's Secret, and, of course, wrist restraints."

MAN SAYS: "I have a great relationship with my dad."

MAN MEANS: "Our monthly phone conversation consists of each of us asking the other how things are going, me saying 'Pretty good, how 'bout yourself?' and him saying, 'Not bad . . . well, talk to you soon. Here's your mother.'"

MAN SAYS: "My last girlfriend and I just grew apart."

MAN MEANS: "You would not believe the bitchy attitude she gave me every time I had to borrow rent money from her!"

MAN SAYS: "I'm feeling some good chemistry here between us."

MAN MEANS: "The sight of your cleavage is giving me thoughts of activities that I'm fairly certain are illegal in at least twelve states."

All right, I'm not so delusional as to think that my dating dictionary is going to completely resolve the big issue of male-female dating communication. But it's a start. And if my little contribution brings just one couple together into a relationship of honest and open communication, genuine friendship, and erotic passion, then it will have all been worth it. All I ask is that they send me the photos—especially the ones featuring the Victoria's Secret outfits and the wrist restraints. Hey, come on, I'm a guy.

Think you've mastered the male lingo? Ready to move on to the advanced level? Great! I just love your enthusiasm!

One out of two marriages end in divorce. Why? I don't know. Ask Tom Cruise. Ask Jim Carrey—for the love of God, ask Al and Tipper Gore. They'll all probably say there was some sort of communication breakdown—which often translates into the man dating someone half his age, losing half his income, and acting like a half-wit.

It all boils down, however, to saying what we mean and being understood. How many times have we told our significant other, "That's not what I meant," "I never said that," "You're misinterpreting my remarks," or even, "Oh, *this* pair of panties that are half your size and stuffed into my glove compartment? It's, um, a gift for you."

In an effort to do my part to improve male-female communication, I've begun writing the *Official Women's Guide to Manspeak*, which serves as an advanced male to female dating dictionary and provides women with actual phrases that men frequently use—and then translates them into what men really mean by them. This guide is based on interviews with thousands of men, plus one very long, agonizing conversation with Roseanne Barr. If I can save just one relationship with my guide, well, then, that's a pretty poor record, but it's a start. Here are some sample entries:

"I'm sorry." I'm not sorry, but I want sex tonight.

"Sweetheart, do we have anything planned for the weekend?" I've made plans to spend the entire weekend drinking and having belching contests with my old fraternity buddies and just wanted to make sure that you hadn't committed us to yet another agonizingly dull function.

"What do you feel like for dinner tonight?" What do you plan to cook for dinner tonight and how fast can you set it in front of me while I watch the sports channel?

"Do you need some help with the housecleaning?" After four straight hours playing video games, I thought I'd poke my head out and ask this at the exact moment I knew you were finished with the cleaning.

"I washed the dishes." Is it sex yet?

"Did you just hear something?" While I continue sleeping, could you go downstairs and check whether or not an escaped felon has broken in? If so, please disarm him and have him arrested, without waking me.

"Of course I'm listening to you." Wow, that girl's not wearing a bra!

"I'm looking for a committed, long-term relationship." I'll say anything I think you need to hear, including this, to get you to take your clothes off.

"Yes, I'd love to go see *Eat, Pray, Love 3* with you." Assuming, that is, that *The A Team 3*, *Iron Man 3*, and *Bipolar Maniacal Killers 3* are sold out.

"No, that's a great look for you, really." Especially if we're going to a costume party and you're supposed to be a house being tented for termites.

"You and your mom look amazingly alike." Oh, God, you're going to end up looking like your mom!

"You think I'm attracted to her? That woman doesn't have one-tenth your class or depth." I would bite off my foot to be with her for one night.

"Your casserole is so unusual and interesting—I have never tasted anything like it." I bet if Fido hadn't eaten for two weeks and I offered this to him, he'd say, "Pass."

"Your sensitivity is one of the things I love most about you." What is it, your time of the month again?

"If I was given the choice between a romantic weekend with you or with Scarlett Johansson, I would choose you." Yeah, right. Anyway, now can we have sex?

"I really want to get into shape this year." My friend at work told me about this new health club that has a coed Jacuzzi.

"Do you think this milk is still good?" Could you taste this disgusting, curdled mess so that I won't have to?

"I run my own business." I approach cars stopped at red lights and squeegee their windows and demand tips.

"After we make love, I just want to hold you." The sooner you fall asleep, the sooner I can scarf down that pizza while watching wrestling on TV.

"Pleased to meet you. My name is Brad Swift." My real name is Shmuel Sapperstein.

"I respect your wanting to remain a virgin until you marry. It shows you have morals and self-control. It'll also make sex more sacred and meaningful when it happens." Check, please!

"I don't think it's either of our faults—we just don't seem to have the right chemistry together." I met a woman with much larger breasts than yours.

"I'm not really in the mood for sex tonight." April Fools!

Shall we move now from the verbal to the physical? (Which, coincidentally, is a first-date line that's never worked for me.) Still, I feel it important to touch upon the all-important concept of eye contact. And, by the way, your eyes are lovely. Yes, I noticed.

Never Underestimate the Importance of Proper Eye Contact

Was it not the great ancient Greek philosopher Aristotle who once posed this timeless question to his disciples: "If a woman on a coffee date seeks a man's undivided attention for her deepest and most penetrating thoughts and feelings, why in Zeus's name would she wear a top with a plunging neckline?"

OK, maybe he didn't say it in exactly those words; perhaps it loses something in translation. OK, maybe it wasn't even the philosopher Aristotle who asked that question; maybe it was his cousin, Sid. Or maybe it's just my problem, but I like to think that perhaps Aristotle had to deal with it, too. Maybe a woman's toga was too loose. In case I run into him in heaven, we'll have something to discuss over a couple of beers. I'd explain to him how last week, I realized as soon as I saw my coffee date, Debra, for the very first time that she had lovely breasts, an enticing portion of which were on clear display, and that it was going to be extremely difficult for me to not be distracted by them, to stay focused on the conversation at hand, and, I'm sorry, what were we talking about?

See, here is one of the major differences between women and men. While Debra was concerned with expressing her innermost feelings, sharing her life story, trying to get a sense of who I was as a fully functional mature human being, I was in a completely different zone—the Breasts Zone. Insensitive? Perhaps. Sexist? No doubt. Juvenile? Probably. Ignorable? No way. While realizing in the back of my mind that words and sounds were emerging from Debra's lips, I would frankly be at a complete loss to let you know what even one of those words or sounds were. Because the front of my brain was busy. It was busy planning strategy. And this is the strategy my brain was attempting to work out with me:

"OK, keep maintaining eye contact with her. Good. That's good; that's real good. She suspects nothing. Now, you see how from time to time she'll break eye contact with you, look away for a few seconds while she continues talking, and then resume eye contact with you? 'Yes.' You don't have to answer; it was a rhetorical question. I'm your brain, dufus; granted, I'm small, tiny actually, but I'm still your brain. Now, you want to get a good look at those breasts, don't you? Of course you do; you're a male. Do you think that during one of those brief moments that she looks away, you could quickly and subtly steal a good look at Debra's breasts, and then just as quickly resume eye contact with her, keeping in mind that if you miscalculate or if she looks back too soon, the shocking image that will be greeting her is you drooling at the sight of her gazongas and then she'll know the real you. She'll know that you're not in this for the soul mate or the life partner or the communication or the sharing or sensitivity. She'll know you're just like all the other guys, one step away from the whistling and hooting construction workers who only care about superficial physical female body parts. You disgust me. If I wasn't your brain, I swear I'd have nothing to do with you."

I start to panic. I start doubting my ability to complete the procedure in the allotted period of time. I'm sure she can see the thin bead of stress sweat forming at the top of my forehead. Suddenly, inexplicably, a different voice from within pipes up with something to calm me down: "Will you relax? She wore that top for a reason. She knows how good she looks and she wants you to enjoy the view. Now, just go ahead and look. Go on. Be natural and casual about it. Do it now. Now. Before it's too late." I wait until Debra looks away. I then steal that glance at her breasts. They're wonderful. As I'm looking at them, my whole life passes before my eyes. And then my life as it could be, together with Debra. And then for some reason, a can of Cheez Whiz.

A feeling of calm and peace comes over me. I am content. I am at one with the universe. Quickly, I return my gaze to Debra's face. She's still looking away, but then turns to meet my gaze. I made it in time. All is well with the world. And then Debra said the words I dreaded hearing, "You were looking at my breasts, weren't you?" I briefly considered denying it, but didn't want to get our relationship off to a dishonest start. "Yes. Yes, I was." And then Debra said the words all men want to hear. "It's okay. You can look all you want." All I could answer was, "Thank you." I dropped my gaze. Wait 'til Aristotle hears this.

Of course, stealing glances at admired body parts isn't the only wordless communication in the world of romance.

Saying It without Words

hen the Vatican chooses a new pope, the traditional white smoke swirls out of the chimney of the Sistine Chapel, the bells of St. Peter's begin to ring, and cheers erupt from the tens of thousands of people in the square below who gather to witness the historic announcement of the next leader of the Roman Catholic Church. It is a moving sight, a beautiful, historical moment. There is something poetic, refreshing, and virtually primal about the use of the symbolic smoke signals and bells in place of a more mundane verbal announcement. It's almost as if a verbal or written announcement would have been inadequate, disappointing, smaller than the grand event it attempted to communicate. The smoke and bells got it just right.

This all begs the question—how many other life events might be more effectively, charmingly, creatively, and appropriately communicated if done so without words? Several come to mind immediately.

Rather than a man hemming and hawing in response to his date's question about whether or not he keeps his place tidy, she could immediately see for herself by the symbolic filthy sock flapping in the breeze atop the flagpole on his house. The doorbell of a National Rifle Association member could be a twenty-one gun salute; what more need be said?

There's no need for high school cafeteria workers to write out a new lunch menu every day. They simply need to set a stomach pump atop the counter. That simple gesture conveys to the students, "Food's ready; yes, it's the same quality and taste you've come to expect each and every day." A guy who's been divorced several times and is basically clueless around women could have a thick red "X" painted across his face, thereby warning unsuspecting women from even blocks away to stay away.

Airline pilots who drink alcohol before takeoff might also show prospective life-loving passengers some consideration by hanging a martini glass–shaped banner from one of the wings.

An earth-shattering, Jamie Lee Curtis horror movie scream of terror could precede any surprise mother-in-law visit. A smoker's household could have on its lawn, instead of a garden gnome, a large sculpture of a black lung perched on a pedestal. And an unemployed son about to pay his parents a visit to ask for a loan could announce his visit, taking a hint from Batman's Bat-Signal in the sky, only this one would be an enormous glowing leech.

If these new nonverbal signals catch on, they could truly save Americans time, energy, and years of learning about the proper response for a given situation. Bosses could literally give fired employees "the boot." Auto mechanics could play

"Taps" to indicate to the car owner the state of his 1978 VW Beetle. And what man receiving a bouquet of dead roses from his girlfriend wouldn't have an exact picture of how she perceives their relationship?

The point is, the world is full of words and we don't need them all. Most of them are just filler. Many are hurtful, even leading to wars. Seventy-eight percent of them are advertising. There are other ways to convey things. Better ways. Let's take a lesson from the papal "announcement," from monks who take vows of silence for years, from mimes, from meditators, from the great silent movies, from animals, from Mother Nature, and from the cosmos.

Thomas Carlyle said, "Under all speech that is good for anything there lies a silence that is better. Silence is deep as Eternity; speech is shallow as Time." Granted, words have their place. This guy Shakespeare did fairly well with them. But every once in a while we might consider putting the words aside, to show rather than tell. Because if you show it the right way, it will tell itself more effectively than words ever could.

Speaking of show and tell, allow me to show you some dating activities that women sometimes suggest—and the reasons why some men aren't overly enthusiastic about them, to put it mildly.

Oh, Come On, It'll Be Fun!

During courtship and dating, women, being the more creative and imaginative gender, will often come up with the majority of suggestions for where they'd like to go and what they'd like to do with their romantic partner. One would think this would be a positive thing. After all, their motivation appears genuine. "Oh, come on, it'll be fun!" they frequently say to us. And yet according to the latest Aw, Jeez, Do I Have To? survey, 96 percent of these suggestions are viewed by us men as embarrassing, boring, or uncomfortable—events and activities in which we would never have chosen to become involved if we were still single. Which leads me to the public service portion of this discourse. Ladies, the following is inside information—a listing of your most common activity suggestions, what we men don't like about them, and what you might instead suggest as nonnauseating substitutes. No, don't thank me; I'm a giver.

CAMPING

Let's take camping, for example. Camping—an activity many men look forward to with the same relish they take in being drafted, reading Aristotle in the original Greek, or attending a Celine Dion concert. The way we see it, nature is way over-rated. How many flowers can you smell? How many sunsets can you see? How many coyotes can you worry about being in the vicinity? No access to the Internet or e-mail. No TV sports. Bugs everywhere. What about any of this spells "fun"? Unless you look at "fun" as the first three letters of "funeral." You want your shot of nature? Invite us to the beach at sunset. Take a blanket and a six-pack, make out for half an hour, and then split. That's enough nature to hold us for the next three months. You want to go camping? Date Smokey the Bear.

OPERA

If given the choice of how to spend a Friday or Saturday night, what guy wouldn't vote for putting on some uncomfortable, formal clothing and spending a couple of hundred dollars, plus another hefty chunk for parking, for tickets to hear some weight-challenged, overcostumed, overly made-up nerds belting out tunes that don't have a beat and don't rhyme, in a language they can't understand? Exactly. But just watch the evil look your girlfriend gives you when you try to stay awake by playing a video game on your cell phone.

If we must do something cultural and uplifting, at least make it ballet, where the women are in shape, wearing form-revealing clothing, and moving their bodies in ways that cause us to imagine them with us in a variety of other nondance situations. As an added bonus, the ballerinas are generally silent and literally "uplifted"—completely willing to be thrown overhead, around the stage, and in a variety of interesting positions. It ain't "Dancing With the Stars," but it sure as hell beats counting down the seconds 'til it's over when the fat lady sings.

TRAVEL

If my extensive online dating experience has taught me nothing else (which may well be the case), it's that, at least according to their dating profiles, the one thing every woman most enjoys—more than food, entertainment, and of course, sex, is—traveling. They all want to get out of the country and see the world, explore other cultures, become enriched and broaden their horizons. These are all noble and worthy pursuits. Men, however, view travel slightly differently. We even spell it differently. We spell it this way: TRAVE$L. We also view it as time away from our jobs. This will virtually guarantee that not only will a huge stack of work be waiting for us upon our return, not only will the boss find out the business runs just fine without our being there, but we'll no doubt come down with some exotic disease and need to be treated by a culture still learning about modern medieval medicine.

Got the travel bug, ladies? That's why God created *National Geographic* magazine. We'll gladly treat you to a subscription.

CLOTHES SHOPPING

Then there's clothing shopping, or as most guys know it better—torture without the sweet release of death. You get to follow your sweetie from store to store with the added bonus of holding her purse as she tries on one dress, blouse, or pair of shoes after another, all afternoon long, lying to her about how each garment does not make her butt look big. Occasionally you meet the eyes of another girl's boyfriend there against his will, and the look you give each other is as though you're both begging, "PLEASE FOR THE LOVE OF GOD PUT ME OUT OF MY MISERY NOW!" At last, you understand why some men in certain situations make the decision to chew their arm off to get away.

You want to try on clothes? Great. Do it at home. We'll light candles, put on some mood music, pour some wine, and you can give us a private fashion show. Oh, sure, it won't be nearly the same without the neon lights, price tags, and glances from other women who think you're a pervert because you're browsing through the lingerie as you wait for your girlfriend to emerge from the dressing room. But it'll be close enough for us.

RELATIONSHIP WORKSHOPS

Naturally, post-divorce, we men are going to want to avoid the mistakes we made during our marriage, not to mention keeping our current romantic relationship as perfectly tuned up as the Kia we're now nearly able to afford after our child-support payments. So, of course we'll welcome the prospect of attending such events as the notorious Rediscovering Intimacy Workshop. Right? Wrong. Holy moly. It's bad enough our intimacy's waning; must we now attempt to jump-start it in a pathetic weekend face-to-face with other romantic losers? We'd rather have a Just Where Do You See This Relationship Going? conversation. We'd rather get in touch with our feelings and cry about what we never got to tell our fathers. We'd rather attend a taping of *Ellen*.

You want to jump-start our intimacy? Make sweet love with us frequently and enthusiastically. You'll be stunned at how rapidly the intimacy returns. In fact, let's start right now. Hey, we went camping with you; it's your turn to do something *we* enjoy. Hey, where are you going? Oh, come on, it'll be fun!

So, even if your romantic partner doesn't enjoy some of the activities you do, could he still be The One? Still be your soul mate? There's only one way to find out—by taking this simple test.

Official Soul Mate Determination Test for Women Only

L adies, how many of your girlfriends would you say are in a blissfully happy romantic relationship with a man they consider to be their soul mate? Exactly. It's rare, if not impossible, with the exception of the relationships in Billy Crystal and Meg Ryan movies, and those aren't even real life, from what I understand.

Which is not to say that you shouldn't feel hopeful that you may one day find your soul mate. For centuries, no one thought we could land on the moon and so, hey, your odds should be at least that good. Just don't bet the farm on it. Especially if you don't have a farm because the mob would come after you and, well, I guess you wouldn't need a soul mate after that. Problem solved, though painfully so.

But let's think positively. At least be prepared for the possibility, otherwise you might not even recognize your soul mate when he comes along. How to prepare? Simply take my Official Soul Mate Determination Test.

Respond honestly and your soul mate will be as clear to you as if he were wearing a T-shirt emblazoned, "I'm Your Soul Mate" on the front and, considering the fact that he's a guy–"NOW can we make love?" on the back.

Ready? OK, you may pick up your pencils, turn your papers over, and begin. Show all work.

1. When you look your potential soul mate in the eyes, you see:
a) Pure, unadulterated love, admiration, and respect.
b) A reddish haze left over from the Summer Bong Fiesta he and his best buddy Willy threw in your honor two days ago.
c) The reflection of the woman he was just with when you showed up to surprise him—as she quickly grabs her lingerie and sneaks out the back door.

2. His affectionate nickname for you is:
a) Goddess.
b) Bee-atch.
c) My Little Bunny Slop.

3. After meeting him for the first time, your mother comments to you:
a) "Where in the world did you find such a perfect, amazing man?"
b) "Honey, don't worry, we'll help you get a restraining order."
c) "That was very thoughtful of Vince to bring along his parole officer."

4. His living quarters remind you of:
a) A page straight out of *Architectural Digest* magazine.
b) The aftermath of Hurricane Ivan.
c) Hell – The Early Years.

5. When you Google his name, you find:
a) Twelve different websites with partial listings of all the humanitarian awards he's been given.
b) Firm warnings from nine women, all suing him for child support.
c) A link to his one published article; OK, self-published article, "Neo-Nazis: America's Misunderstood Minority."

6. As a special treat for your birthday, he surprised you with:
a) 100 roses and a mariachi band serenading you outside your window.
b) A trip to the National Motorcycle & Tattoo Show.
c) $5,000, fresh from the 7-Eleven safe.

SCORING

Well, there's your trouble right there. If you're still into "scoring," you're most likely not even ready for a soul mate relationship. So, go on; get it out of your system. You're only young once, unless you believe in reincarnation, in which case perhaps you'll return as a young hamster, which brings with it its own unique soul mate problems. But I digress. The point is, like you need me to tell you this, there's no test in the world that can determine who your soul mate might be. Like brushing your teeth and egging your vice-principal's car, it's something you're just going to have to handle on your own. You'll no doubt feel it when it's right. And if he never comes along? Well, that's why God created movies and Häagen-Dazs.

Think positive, though. Say he comes along and you're lucky enough to hit it off and end up having a world-class, passionate romance. Just one question—what do you talk about in bed?

If only there was some sort of user's manual for that sort of thing.

Pillow Talk:
A User's Guide

Take a stroll through your local bookstore and you'll find self-help guides telling you what to say during a job interview, a funeral, a corporate speech, a language lesson, a tax audit, a police arrest, even a conversation with a dolphin. Nowhere, however, will you find even one paragraph describing what might be appropriate to say to your lover while making love. Hence the need for my hopefully-soon-to-be-in-bookstores-despite-having-been-rejected-by-over-100-publishers guide, *Pillow Talk: Yes, Yes, God, Yes!*

The book is based on the candid replies of hundreds of men and women who filled out my intimate survey in exchange for sending them my Grandma Rivka's secret recipe for Matzoh Ball Ice Cream Cake Supreme with Kosher Sprinkles. It's a surefire crowd-pleaser and is just as good, if not better, the next day. But I digress.

First of all, a rather surprising finding: A substantial portion of the lovemaking population apparently doesn't talk at all during sex. The feeling seems to be that: 1) They're too exhausted from having already done all that talking to convince the other one to have sex. 2) They might miss one of Jimmy Fallon's monologue jokes. 3) The process of fantasizing about Brad Pitt and Scarlett Johansson could be ruined by hearing one another's actual voices, which are invariably closer to those of Tom Waits and Phyllis Diller.

Of those who do talk, however, the words "I love you" are among the most popular terms of endearment. Coming in close behind them are "I want you," "I need you," and "Do that again, only this time a little slower and this time could I be the chain gang leader and you be the brand-new virginal convict?"

Complimenting one's lover is also a very common technique. Frequently employed compliments include: "Your body is so beautiful," "You are so smart," and "I get so hot when you describe yourself as a warlock and a rock star from Mars."

Sometimes, a problem weighs so heavily upon one's mind that it needs to be discussed even during sex. In such cases, the other partner should be sympathetic and supportive, offering such responses as, "I agree, honey—the Geneva Peace Talks are being horribly mishandled. If they could only be handled as well as you're handling me right now, the world would be a safer place. Oh, God, do that again."

Other times, the mood may be so light and carefree that loving little nicknames seem the most appropriate things that could be uttered: "You're my little peach cobbler," "You're my big mountain explorer," and "You're my rack and pinion steering gear." (This last one popular primarily among auto mechanics and guys named Wade.)

There are certain areas deemed inappropriate for bedroom conversation. Topping the list is the phrase, "Good Lord, what is that thing on your back!?" Equally mood-shattering is any kind of request for a loan, any attempt to make a citizen's arrest, or a tattoo indicating the professional sports teams serviced during "a very confusing time for me, but I swear it will never happen again, and a lot of times I don't even write them back when they send me requests for my panties, so quit making such a big deal about it, Wade."

Poetry has long held nearly aphrodisiacal qualities when employed properly—that is, when it truly comes from the heart. Which is not to say that verse along the lines of, "There once was a young lad from Venus..." would not yield romantic results. It's just that there are more eloquent and sophisticated poetic techniques that should be explored before resorting to, "Roses are red; violets are blue; sugar is sweet; I want to hop on you."

One of the keys to successful bedroom conversation for lovers is gratitude. It is so important to continually show one's gratitude to one's partner. This can take many forms, including this classic oldie but goody: "Oh, Mr. President, never mind about my blue dress—I'm just honored to be here!"

Another important key to keep in mind is acknowledgment and acceptance of your partner's differences: "I really love how when you become most excited, you make the sound of a World War II German ambulance siren . . . Wade."

As you can see, there are a whole world of ways to communicate while making love. The important thing is to be true to yourself and really share what you feel with your partner. I myself enjoy sharing the true story of the time my Uncle Benny trimmed his chest hair into a recreation of Moses leading his

Relationships 101

Not to put a damper on the romantic month of February, but just to keep things realistic and in perspective—we've all heard that one out of two marriages ends in divorce. Countless books, videos, seminars, and therapists exist to serve those in dysfunctional romantic relationships. And for those of us who are single, good luck finding someone with whom you'd even want to be in a romantic relationship.

Why is finding and sustaining a successful romantic relationship so difficult? I blame the American education system. It teaches us a world of information we most likely will never need unless we're either settling a bar bet, appearing on *Jeopardy*, or helping our children with their obscure, fact-laden homework. By the time I graduated from college, I knew an impressive amount about Ancient Greek history, subtext in Shakespeare's *Richard III*, and a frog's intestines. Don't ask me when I last used any of it.

As for creating and sustaining a romantic relationship, though—I pretty much knew, and still know, squat. Why do we spend so much time and energy teaching our children so much Trivial Pursuit-like "stuff" while disregarding vital life skills they so desperately need? All that's going to change when I become Czar of Education. You can bet that changing a tire, balancing a checkbook, and cooking a meal will be part of my curriculum. And there will especially be a wide variety of courses available dealing with romantic relationships, including the following, taken directly from my proposed Relationships 101 syllabus:

GEOGRAPHY OF ROMANCE – A course dealing with the best places to meet your romantic partner. Certain locales lend themselves to greater relationship success—churches and temples, the homes of friends and relatives, bookstores, supermarkets, restaurants, parks, and beaches. Other places tend to be riskier—prison, tattoo parlors, methamphetamine labs, mosh pits, wife-swapping parties, Chuck E. Cheese's restaurants, gatherings of arms dealers. You can't find the Wow unless you know the Where. But enough quoting Aristotle.

INTERROGATORY LAND MINES – These refer to specific questions your romantic partner will be asking you. The most important thing to remember is that any response you give, no matter how carefully considered, how sensitive, or how loving, will anger your partner and put your relationship at risk. Such questions include, "Do you think our waitress is pretty?" "If I died tonight, which of my girlfriends would you most want to date?" and, of course, the ever-popular, "Does this dress make me look fat?" Learn invaluable techniques for changing the subject, distracting with compliments, and faking a seizure.

HANDLING REJECTION – Why you still have value as a human being despite being turned down as a romantic partner. Why a woman who turns you down may not necessarily be a lesbian. Why a man who turns you down may not necessarily have a fear of commitment—he just may not want to commit to you. Why when your romantic partner says "I'm not in the mood," it does not mean you have a license to leave the house angrily and find someone who is in the mood. (Trust me.) Why the fact that your dog is your only true friend may not necessarily be a bad thing. For the dog, that is.

HANDLING REJECTION II: INAPPROPRIATE RESPONSES TO BEING DUMPED – Guest lecturers who have actually either made or received these inappropriate responses will discuss: keying his car, posting embarrassing nude photos of her on the Internet, committing ritual Japanese suicide (appearing via video made shortly before his demise), weeping loudly and completely out of context for months, burning down his house, kidnapping his children, reporting her to the Department of Homeland Security, and losing interest in everything in life except the reality show *Dancing with the Stars*. Bitter students with an axe to grind are more than welcome.

THINGS TO MAKE SURE YOUR ROMANTIC PARTNER DOESN'T SEE THE FIRST TIME SHE VISITS YOUR HOUSE – For men only. The first part of the course will identify those things that most men are unaware ticks women off, including: dirty dishes in the sink, dirty underwear on the floor, dirty dishes on the floor, dirty underwear in the sink, other women in the bed, other men in the bed. (Sorry, I just saw *Brokeback Mountain*). The second part of the course will deal with methods you can use to salvage the relationship once she is completely grossed out by your disgusting habitat. In addition, each student receives a complimentary subscription to *Martha Stewart Living*; a clothes hamper; and a huge, scent-concealing empty box into which you can dump all your dirty clothing and dishes until you have the time and energy to deal with them.

Now, you gotta admit—all that is education you can use. And speaking of education, here's one test I'll bet you were never given in school. I created it for my fellow Jews, but I'm positive you can create your own version for any religion.

Test-a-Jew

Back in high school, I had a crush on a Protestant girl, Joan Reid. She told me that her mother encouraged her to date—and even marry—Jewish guys because: a) They're smarter and work harder; b) They make great fathers; c) They don't get drunk and beat you. I told Joan her mom was absolutely correct, and then spent the rest of the year attempting to leverage that information into getting Joan's bra off. But I digress.

The fact of the matter is, Jewish men are in demand, not just among Jewish women, but among non-Jewish women as well. Similarly, there are non-Jewish men who have a thing for Jewish women. All well and good. The problem is that some of these gentiles are signing up on Jewish singles sites like JDate and raiding our people. They're going Hebrew fishing.

Oh, sure, some of these "pretenders to the faith" will admit up front that they're not Jewish, but many will not. It's false advertising. Bait and switch. They'll get a Jewish man or woman to fall in love with them, and only then reveal their dark secret. Shame! But, assuming this matters to you, what can be done about this treachery? Nothing. How can one determine if said potential romantic partner is, in fact, a Jew? One can't. That is, one couldn't—until now.

Fellow Jewish singles, no longer will a non-Jew take advantage of your good will and trusting nature. No longer will non-Jews toy with your affections. No longer will you give yourself, body and soul, to an, for want of a better word, Episcopalian, only to find out that he or she grew up in a household in which the only time "Jew" was even mentioned was in conjunction with the terms "devil horns," "owning show business" and "killing our Lord."

Yes, our days and nights of uncertainty and betrayal are over. For, as a public service to my faith, I have created a foolproof means of determining whether your potential life partner is one of the Chosen People. Now, admittedly, I am still perfecting and fine-tuning my Test-a-Jew creation. But, just to get you started, here is a brief sampling. Feel free to try them on your dates. But I beg you, if they answer incorrectly, can't answer correctly immediately, or get a glazed look in their eyes, run!

Test-a-Jew Sample Questions
1) Abba is:
a. The secret code word for getting into the hottest Bar Mitzvah parties.
b. A Swedish band famous for cheesy music that's still popular, God knows why.
c. The Hebrew word for "father."

2) Mezuzah is:

a. The personal form of "Youzuzah."

b. A small parchment scroll written by a scribe and affixed to the doorpost containing the first two paragraphs of the Shema.

c. The sound made in the throat when ingesting a blintz that's too dry.

3) "Gut Shabbos" is an expression meaning:

a. Good Sabbath.

b. Shabby Guts.

c. We still own show business—pass it on.

4) Which of the following sentences uses the word *shpilkes* properly?

a. Did you shave your *shpilkes* today?

b. I had *shpilkes* before my big job interview.

c. Would you prefer some of the chocolate or the coconut *shpilkes*?

5) Which of these best describes Haman?

a. The villain of the story of Purim.

b. The last name of the one Orthodox Jew who plays professional hockey.

c. The menu term immediately preceding "cheese sandwich."

6) Kashrut is:

a. The condition immediately preceding bankruptcy.

b. Jewish dietary laws.

c. His real last name before he became "Neil Diamond."

I think you'll agree with me that a test like this will do much to weed out the Jew-pretenders. If this situation is left unchecked, trust me, one day you'll wake up to find your kids have blond hair, straight noses, and think a schnorrer is someone who makes a lot of noise in his sleep.

Of course, once you've identified your date as Jewish, you'll want to know how to seduce said Jew. Here's how I do it. Feel free to borrow, improvise, come up with your own personalized version, turn me in to the authorities—whatever seems right.

How to Seduce
a Jewish Woman

There are 613 commandments in Leviticus, but tonight let us just focus on two of our own commandments—for me to love you and for you to love me. The Messiah is coming in the future to take us to Israel, the land of milk and honey. While we're waiting, why not enjoy each other's milk and honey? After all, I've been a man since my thirteenth birthday. You've been a woman since your twelfth. We've had years of practice being a man and a woman. Let's show each other what we've learned. Let's have a hot night of Judaic show and tell.

We Jews do not believe in original sin, the concept that all people have inherited Adam and Eve's sin when they disobeyed God's instructions in the Garden of Eden. No, we believe we were born perfect and only later in life face temptation and sin. Tonight's our night for temptation and sin, my little hamentashen. For here we are at last, my little kugel, facing one another unashamed, because in Jewish law, sex is not considered shameful, sinful, or obscene. In Judaism, sex is not merely a way of experiencing physical pleasure. It is an act of immense significance, which requires commitment and responsibility. The requirement of marriage before sex ensures that sense of commitment and responsibility. That is why I have asked Rabbi Bernstein to join us here tonight. "You can come in now, Rabbi!" He will marry us now, and then, my darling, he will leave and we will take each other to the Promised Land.

Now that we've covered the religious aspects of dating, let's continue into the political realm. Disclaimer: I know virtually nothing about politics. Of course, that hasn't stopped many of our nation's political leaders from running for office, so I'm okay with that.

Interpolitical Dating Tips

There aren't many outstanding "interpolitical" couples we can look up to. In the past, we could have cited Republican Arnold Schwarzenegger and Democrat Maria Shriver as peaceful partners, but they've since said "hasta la vista, baby." Arnold's back making movies and Maria's no doubt back dating human-sized men.

The most high-profile couple with opposing political beliefs (that is still together) is Democratic strategist James Carville and Republican consultant Mary Matalin. The two were married in 1993, one year after they had staffed opposing presidential campaigns, and have said they don't talk politics at home. (Which is probably a good idea for relationship longevity for couples on opposite sides of various spectrums—not to talk politics, religion, or which of your spouse's friends or relatives you would "do" if given the opportunity).

So what about us normal folk—the people who don't make a living working and breathing politics but still have opinions on the issues? Here are some additional tips on how to keep the peace with a partner of a different political party:

- Don't bring it up: What's the first rule of Fight Club? "Don't talk about Fight Club." Politics can be just as brutal—though you usually don't have to wear a protective cup.

- Agree to disagree: Even if we like to think of ourselves as "open-minded," most of us have our minds made up about major political issues. Your efforts to change your partner's mind will not only be unsuccessful, but could result in having heavy objects thrown at your head in a heated fight. You can often spot such people walking down the street. They're the ones with omelet pans embedded in their skulls. Just smile understandingly and say, "I know . . . I know."

- Focus on the positive: Your partner must have some other redeeming qualities besides his or her politics, right? After all, Albert Einstein and the Kardashians were able to carve out entire careers without mentioning politics, and how often do you even hear their names in the same sentence? Instead of emphasizing your differences, focus on your shared hobbies and opinions. Some middle-of-the-road interests to get you started: pizza, football, puppies, The Beatles, light bondage. You know, those sorts of things.

- Be up front: Sure, lies are fun and exciting, and lying gives you a thrill that nothing else can match, but . . . where was I going with this? Oh, yeah—be honest with your significant other about your beliefs, and be honest with yourself about how important those beliefs are to you. And, of course, be honest about how that spanking the other night was just a tad more painful than you'd expected. Or am I just bringing up too much of my own experience here?

- Be respectful: Making fun of other people is great—but not when you're trying to develop a relationship. You don't have to agree with one another, but at least don't belittle the other person's beliefs. So, get in the habit of saying things like, "While I don't share your feelings about Mitt Romney, I respect them."

- Share the TiVo: Don't watch Bill Maher in front of your partner if he or she is a Bill O'Reilly fan. DVR all your favorite programs and sneak out of bed to watch them in the middle of the night while your partner sleeps. Or, watch clips online at work like a real American. Or, use those shows as punishment for one another. If she overcooks or burns dinner, she must watch an episode of Bill Maher's show. If you forget her birthday, get ready to watch Bill O'Reilly's.

- Show your true colors: If you're really itching to show your pride, passive-aggressively support your political party by wearing red or blue garb. Your significant other will never know that you are secretly campaigning, and if they call you out, you can make THEM look crazy. "OMG you can't even look at the color red without thinking of Sarah Palin?!?" This is a technique known as "gaslighting"—making someone think that they are actually going crazy. And romantic relationships don't get much more fun than that.

- If all else fails, cut and run: Americans only get worked up about politics every four years (or two, if you're a midterm person). Tell your partner you've been called out of town on business until November 9. That will give him or her a few days after the election to stop gloating and/or crying. Meanwhile you can sip drinks by the pool in sunny Canada. Dysfunctional? Of course. What's your point?

Politics aside, a wise person once said that the four most important words a man can use to ensure longevity in a relationship are "I'm sorry" and "Yes, dear." Although I'm also a big fan of flowers and an evening of lovemaking. Just be sure that neither the flowers nor the bedsheets are red, white, and blue. Finally, since I am a man, or so I'm told, I'd like to leave my male readers with a little gift. No, it's not Scarlet Johansson's phone number, but good guess. Rather, it's something I think you'll ultimately find much more valuable. Consider it a supportive warning.

Psssst, Men—Beware of These Potential Dating Disasters

There are men who manage to go through their entire dating lives without stress, anxiety, failure, offending anyone or being offended, rejecting anyone or being rejected, without encountering even one dating dilemma or disaster. They, instead, have smooth, successful, joyous, passionate, love-filled, worry-free dating lives without incident. Do such men really exist? Yes! Do they truly have such idyllic dating lives? Indeed they do. Can you find them on online dating sites? Sadly, no. Then, who are these men? Well, as it turns out, they're called—fictitious characters. You'll find them in books, plays, TV shows and movies, but you certainly won't find them in real life because they are fantasy figures, much like Zeus, Harry Potter, or a viable presidential candidate.

Yes, all of us who date encounter, from time to time, bumps of one size or another on the Highway of Love. And there's nothing said about traversing it in the Department of Motor Vehicles booklet. It's part of the relationship package. Perhaps the positive aspect of these love bumps is that they serve to make us even more appreciative of the *good* dating experiences. Still, it never hurts to be on alert for any potential dating disasters that could be lurking around the corner. So, as a public service to my gender, here are a couple of potential dating disasters for men, along with a suggestion or two about dealing with them.

1. Online Dating "Bait and Switch"

Bait and switch is a form of fraud, most commonly used in retail sales but also applicable to other contexts. First, customers are "baited" by advertising for a product or service at a low price; second, the customers discover that the advertised good is not available and are "switched" to a costlier product. Substitute "attractive dating prospect" for "low price," and "less desirable dating prospect" for "costlier product," and you have the form of bait and switch that frequently occurs in the online dating world. And to be fair, both women and men are perpetrators and victims. So guys, don't be surprised if that thirty-five-year-old single Pilates instructor with an average build and her own home turns out to be a forty-eight-year-old separated waitress with the physique of a linebacker, living with her mom, along with her three hyperactive kids and two cats with intestinal problems. Lesson: Ensure the photos are current and the information absolutely accurate. I speak from personal experience—I'm still trying to get those cat stains off my carpet.

2. Every Breath You Take, Every Move You Make, She'll Be Watching You

Why? Because she's just so crazy about you that she wants to be with you every moment of every day, if not in person, then via phone or e-mail. The truth? She's just plain crazy! I actually had a girlfriend who thought it was strange that when we were together, I felt the need to close the bathroom door while I was using the bathroom. She felt that when you're intimate with someone, you should share everything, including the sights and sounds of relieving yourself, grooming yourself, etc. Good lord, how about keeping a shred of mystery in the relationship?! How about an occasional evening to yourself? How about not feeling that the only way to gain a little independence and privacy is to take out a restraining order?! Explain it to her that way. She'll understand. Then escort her gently out of the bathroom.

3. Spending $100 to find out you never want to see her again.

Not that I'm psychic or anything, (though one woman once referred to me as "psycho") or have any special mental powers, but I can generally tell within the first five minutes of meeting a woman for the first time whether there's at least the potential for a relationship. And I've heard plenty of women saying they have this "gift," too. It has something to do with physical attraction, chemistry, and little subtle things such as her touching my thigh while whispering, "I want you." And since that wonderful mutual attraction is the exception rather than the rule, does it make economic sense to spend, on a first date, up to $100 on a restaurant meal with drinks when odds are you will never see this woman again? Especially if you date fairly regularly. And your last name is not Gates or Trump. That's why we have the term "coffee date" and why coffee dates are so widespread and popular.

Yet women will sometimes steer men to agreeing to meet for dinner, or appetizers and drinks, which can be nearly as costly depending on where you go. Women will say, "I don't drink coffee or tea." "I prefer alcoholic beverages." Or, they're only available to meet at exactly lunch or dinner time. Don't do it! Stand firm! A lovely restaurant atmosphere and a full belly will never compensate for a lack of chemistry. But there I go quoting Aristotle again. You'll only end up resenting her and the void in your wallet. So, meet her on the weekend, at a juice bar, suggest a walk in the park or at a beach or museum. Or running through fields of daisies in slow motion, like in the movies. Otherwise, not only will it turn out to be an agonizingly long evening with someone in whom you immediately know you have no interest, but it will require your taking on a second job to afford what you'll end up spending on regular first-meeting restaurant dates. Trust me. And if things work out between the two of you, you'll have plenty of future opportunities for being a big spender. You're welcome.

SECTION THREE:
DATING FANTASIES

I Finally Found the Perfect Woman

February 12, 2004—a day I will never forget. It was on that day that Mattel announced that Barbie—the world's most famous doll—and Ken, her boyfriend, were splitting up. Little girls everywhere mourned the demise of their favorite doll's romance. But like most single men, the news that Barbie and Ken had grown apart and were going their separate ways thrilled me in ways a perfectly prepared plate of lox and eggs never could. Why? Simple. Like most men, I wanted her. Yes, I'll admit it openly and unashamedly—I wanted Barbie with the white-hot intensity of a thousand suns.

Well, come on, who wouldn't want Barbie? Talk about being a multitasker! She's a successful businesswoman, lead singer in a rock band, World Cup soccer player, top fashion model, doctor, astronaut, police officer, presidential candidate, and UNICEF volunteer—not to mention that perfect face and body. Personally, I always think of her as she was first created—in a ponytail and zebra-striped bathing suit, open-toed shoes, sunglasses, and earrings. Oh, Barbie. My perfect woman. Yummy.

Due to my sensitive and considerate nature, however, I had far too much respect for Barbie's feelings to pounce on her right after the announcement of her breakup. Having endured the pain of breakups before, I understood the need to give the person space and time for the healing process. And so I waited. I waited well over two years. Almost 800 days of consideration on my part and healing on Barbie's. Clearly, the time was ripe to make my move. I was a man on a love mission, and Barbie was the one and only target.

Through a publicist friend, I managed to get ahold of Barbie's home phone number. Still, it took me a month and several glasses of Merlot to summon up the courage to call. Surprisingly, she picked up the phone herself. Her voice thrilled me. It was sort of a mixture of Lauren Bacall and Betty Boop. After I made some awkward small talk, asking about Kelly and Skipper and Christie, the conversation finally got around to dating and relationships. Barbie was remarkably friendly and open, revealing that she'd finally come to terms with Ken's inability to commit to the relationship and take the next step toward marriage.

After some prodding, Barbie shared that Ken had admitted to her that he is gay and had just been using her to advance his own career and to avoid coming out of the closet. We both agreed that we disliked that kind of dishonesty, especially at the expense of another's feelings. Here, Barbie's voice choked up a little. As much as she enjoyed having a steady relationship, she had, after all, spent 45 years in love with an in-denial gay man. That had to cause some emotional wounds.

I offered my sympathy and understanding, and suggested that perhaps it was time for her to move on with her romantic life—to a heterosexual man determined to make her every day a passion-filled paradise. She liked that. I remember her exact words: "I like that." We arranged to meet for dinner at a charming little French bistro.

When Barbie arrived at the bistro, she took my breath away. Granted, she's small. Some jealous women have even accused her of being a little too plastic and a little too perfect. But not to me. Barbie is stunning in person. Add to that a sparkling personality, refreshing humility and self-deprecation, delightful sense of humor, refreshing sense of curiosity about everything and everyone, and a perfectly coordinated outfit, and, well, I fell even more deeply in love with her.

The five hours we spent conversing at the dinner table flew by in what seemed like ten minutes. (Incidentally, don't let her tiny dimensions fool you—the woman eats like a horse!) We talked about everything—our hopes, our dreams, our fears, dating gay men who pretend to be heterosexual. At the end of the evening, Barbie unexpectedly asked if I'd like to have a drink at her place. I'm generally one to take things slowly, but you try resisting Barbie.

An hour later, we were in bed. And although I'm not one to kiss and tell, let me simply say that Barbie is a passionate, generous, insatiable lover. She's also, frankly, more than a little kinky. It was her idea that we play her favorite fantasy game—The Cheerleader and the Lumberjack. I was Sven and she was Debbi. She has spoiled me for all other women, and I simply cannot get her out of my mind.

Barbie and I have been together every night since we met and seem to be falling deeper in love each day. We've even double-dated with Ken and G.I. Joe—two other people who can't seem to keep their hands off each other. Do we have problems? Sure. My family doesn't approve of our dating. And we get some strange looks when we're out dancing since I have to clip her onto my belt buckle so she doesn't get trampled. But, hey, what relationship doesn't have its challenges? And anyway, we're both so happy together, taking things one day at a time, even discussing having children. So at least for now, ladies, I'm off the dating market—and deliriously fulfilled in the arms of a real doll.

There Truly is Someone for Everyone

"*Romantic, sensitive, sincere, caring, honest, affection-ate 25-year-old nonsmoking male, a Brad Pitt look-alike with great sense of humor, PhD. in business, runs own advertising agency, enjoys sports, nature, movies, theater, restaurants, dancing—seeks sincere woman for lifelong romance.*"

Dear Romantic: My heart skipped a beat when I read your personals profile on Soulmates4Ever.com because it pretty much described my ideal man. So even though I'm sure you'll be overwhelmed with responses, here's mine: I'm a bright, honest, loving, considerate, vivacious, outgoing 23-year-old blonde, shapely, nonsmoking female, often described as a Katie Holmes look-alike. I am independently wealthy, and love exotic travel, gourmet cooking, and passionate embraces in front of a roaring fire. Please check out my profile. I am yearning for your reply. —StunningOne

Dear StunningOne: Thank you for your wonderful e-mail in response to my profile. Coincidentally, you described my ideal woman. Unfortunately, I wasn't exactly 100 percent honest about myself in my profile. But your message touched me to such a degree that I've decided to stop deluding myself and others. So even though it may cost me the loss of meeting you, here's the truth: I'm a forty-six-year-old Shrek look-alike who smokes like a chimney, dropped out of high school to steal cars, still lives with my parents, and haven't the slightest idea how to function in a social situation.

Dear Romantic: I can't tell you how relieved I was to receive your refreshingly honest response. I, too, have had it with all the artifice, the game-playing, the misrepresentation. So please allow me to revise my initial profile information as well: I'm a fifty-two-year-old, enormously overweight woman, interested solely in my next meal. I suffer from indescribable body odor, but it doesn't bother me too much as I spend most of my days dealing with the voices I hear, commanding me to do the bidding of Borgar, ruler of my home planet. I am currently working gutting fish at Harvey's Carp-O-Rama, but it's the evening shift, so I have my days free to tend to my open sores and seventeen cats. I also like looking in people's windows while drooling.

Dear StunningOne: Your candor touched me to my soul, so please allow me to continue sharing myself with you in preparation for our eventual meeting. I have several rare skin diseases which have been written up in medical journals worldwide. I am allergic to almost all foods, with the exceptions of brussels sprouts; beans; and loose, runny cheeses. The high point of my day is putting on one of those orange school crossing guard vests and nothing else, and helping small children cross the street. I also enjoy setting fires and weeping out of context.

Dear Romantic: I am not allowed to leave my city, for reasons I cannot disclose until the year 2025. Most nights, I wrap myself in large Hefty bags and run up and down the stairs either yodeling or screaming at the various bacteria that invariably come to life and take on human form. I know they're conspiring against me, but I will be triumphant. My parents tried to have me put away, but I fixed them so that they won't be giving me too much trouble any more, if you catch my drift. Sometimes I feel restless and howl at the sun for hours, but that could just be the woman in me. I itch like the dickens in unspeakable places.

Dear StunningOne: I am working on a plan to break Charles Manson out of jail. He's always been a close friend, and I know the three of us will make a great team. Slowing down the process is the fact that I have completely lost control of my bowels. Funny how you don't really appreciate something until it starts acting up. Say, what does it mean when your hair starts coming out in huge clumps? I've enclosed some for your inspection, along with some other assorted body fluids, etc. Can't wait to meet you at Starbucks this weekend.

Dear Romantic: It was really great meeting you for the first time last night. I can't believe we're actually going to elope at the end of the month! Emperor Borgar would just die if he found out! But you have proven to me that there's somebody out there for everyone, that my life means something to someone, and that, thank God, true romantic love really does exist!

Just Another Fairy Tale Romance

Anyone who met him realized he was far from a special man. Seven hundred and twelve miles away, to be exact. His voice was light, trivial, like a thistle bloom falling into silence without a sound, without any weight, as though a parakeet was being vacuumed out of its cage. His lifelong projectile phlegm problem didn't help matters.

Still, there was a manly aroma about him. It was the lusty odor of earth and cattle, mixed with the scent of Parisian nightlife and never-washed junior high school sneakers. He smelled tart and fruity and full of vitamin C, yet there was also the nauseating stench of low tide and crawling things and badly prepared Szechuan eggplant. And, of course, there was his beloved tattoo—the one of the transvestite bikers convention where his parents had met.

Yes, he was a complex man, and it was exactly this complexity which compelled him this day to ride the city bus dressed in his Weinerschnitzel counterperson's uniform which, he proudly noted, still fit him from high school, when the fast-food restaurant was called Der Weinerschnitzel. Yes, they had removed the "Der." It was now simply Weinerschnitzel. But why had they removed the "Der"? Too Germanic? Once you have Weinerschnitzel, though, how much more Germanic does "Der" make it? If it were up to him, he'd bring back the "Der." Der Weinerschnitzel. It sounded more authentic than just Weinerschnitzel. But, hey, they must have their reasons.

A firm voice nudged him out of his musings. It was the bus driver, shouting in his ear, "For the last time, get off my lap!"

As he moved to another seat, it occurred to him that time is the wind that blows down life's corridors, slamming all the doors. Oh, sure, you could open the doors back up, but they all had those annoying hinges that make them close automatically. And just try complaining to the manager, that flour-faced elfin man whose arms looked like they'd been squeezed from tubes. That gave him an idea for a song he could write. He'd call it "That Flour-Faced Elfin Man Whose Arms Looked Like They'd Been Squeezed From Tubes." Maybe he'd even add a "Der" to it.

It was then that he noticed her. She was a big, ripe-bodied blonde with all the bloom of youth, and yet deliriously dull and bovine at the same time. Here, he thought, was a woman who could no doubt do what only the most exquisite, desirable women could—throw a softball like a cannon shot. She was a lovely, skillfully made, richly evocative woman, yet one who might also be referred to as a "pig."

He could feel across the bus the surging power of her presence. Or was it that Burrito Grande with grilled peppers and extra beans he had wolfed down for lunch? In any case, he loved the curve of her mouth, the gentleness of her eyes, the graceful strength of her hands which clutched the *Soldier of Fortune* magazine she read while munching on a Hostess Ding Dong and laughing completely out of context. *My goddess*, he thought. *My dear goddess . . . My der goddess.*

Suddenly, she looked up and when her eyes met his, her heart thudded like a drum. She gave her pacemaker a whack, which returned her heartbeat to its normal Cajun rhythm. There was something she instinctively liked about him. Was it the fluid, rippling motion of his muscles, his rakish good looks, or was it the fact that the freckles on his face spelled out the phrase, "I own a Ferrari"?

She flushed as a rush of warmth splashed over her and then informed the drunk beside her that this was not a public restroom. She got up and went to sit beside the object of her sudden passions. A trembling thrill raced through her as he informed her that the main interests of his life were pleasuring women and finding discount socks.

She was a little in awe of him, confused by his easy charm and by the fact that he was squeezing out the contents of a can of Cheez Whiz on her Converse high-tops. They conversed for hours, sharing everything. He confided that he ran a chain of imaginary time-share vacation condos on the Riviera. She showed him her tattoo of sports legend Marv Alpert being treated at the Betty Ford Clinic.

Later, back at his place, his fingers fumbled with the buttons of her sweater. There were ninety-seven buttons—one, she said, for each time the vice squad had named her Catch of the Day. Her body, alive now, yearned for a conqueror, but he was only up to button number twenty-six and insisted upon singing a German beer hall song every five buttons. And while his rendition of "The Kaiser's Hunting March" was among the best she'd ever heard, she sensed it might be a long night.

Impatient, she tore her sweater off herself, wanting to unleash his hunger and satisfy it, despite the fact that he was now stuffing his face with Chef Boyardee Beef Ravioli, while giggling at a rerun of *SpongeBob SquarePants*. Ever the thoughtful gentleman, he offered her the last ravioli. He finally finished and moved against her, caressing her body with the one remaining piece of garlic bread he hadn't scarfed down. No one had done that to her since the Feast of San Gennaro.

Her hands sledded over the muscles of his back, tobogganed down his torso, and finished with an impressive luge down his legs. For her efforts, she received a 9.2, 8.7, and 9.8, which bested her Tokyo records by a full half-point.

And so it became a sweet, fairy tale romance that seemed too fragile for the real world. He knew in his heart and soul that this was the loveliest, most fulfilling experience of his life, despite the fact that she would later sell their story to the tabloids and kept whispering "Bastard!" behind his back.

The Continuing Adventures of Shlomo Rabinowitz: Jewish Private Eye & Dating Specialist

I t was a warm April afternoon—the kind of afternoon that said, "Kick off your shoes, pick up the Talmud, pour yourself a cup of borscht with a dollop of sour cream, and while the day away." But I was not to have the relaxing pleasure of that kind of afternoon. Not that day. For there was a knock at the door. Oh, by the way, my name is Rabinowitz. Shlomo Rabinowitz. And I'm a JPE—Jewish Private Eye. My specialty? Affairs of the heart.

I opened the door and gasped. Her beauty took my breath away, sucker punched it, put it through a wind tunnel, juggled it, and tossed it back into my lungs. She was 5 feet 4 inches of Hebraic heaven. "Detective Shlomo Rabinowitz?" she inquired with a voice like liquid velvet mixed with blintzes. My mouth opened to answer in the affirmative, yet nothing came out. "My name is Rivka Blatberg," she purred. Rivka Blatberg. It was the kind of name that evoked visions of soft hands moving above

Shabbos candles, passionate days on a kibbutz, feeding one another chocolate dreidels. It was the kind of name that made grown rabbis grow weak in the knees.

I motioned her inside and watched her as she walked toward the chair. I envied the form-fitting garment that hugged each curve of her Judaic form. She had the kind of face for which you'd gladly miss your nephew's Bar Mitzvah to be near. And a body that could take you to the Land of Milk and Honey (and certain portions of New Jersey.) As she sat down, I found myself envying her chair as I asked her how I could be of service.

"Mr. Rabinowitz, I understand you're the best Jewish private eye dating specialist in town," she said. "Please—Shlomo," I offered. "And I'm flattered that my reputation precedes me. You've obviously seen my commercials on local cable—'If your heart's going 'Oh, no!' come see Shlomo.'"

Rivka then got to the point, her eyes welling up with tears like the Red Sea at high tide. "You've got to help me find him, Shlomo!" "Find whom, Rivka? The man who done you wrong? The man who robbed your innocence? The man who stole your heart and vanished like the last rugelach on the plate at an Overeaters Anonymous meeting?" She shook her head no. "It's not like that, Shlomo. You see, I've never even met him." "Never met him?" I responded. "Why, that's more meshugenah than Lady Gaga at a Hadassah meeting. How can I find someone you've never met?"

She looked directly into my eyes. I made a mental note to take several cold showers later. "Shlomo, I've never been in love, and I want so desperately to care for a man and for him to care for me. I want you to find me a man to love." I sighed, and as I did so, I could make out the lingering aroma of the whitefish and kugel I'd had for lunch.

"Rivka, I'm no matchmaker."

"Please, Shlomo, you know so much about romance. You know so many people. It's your occupation. You live it and breathe it. Work with me. Find me my beshert."

I was about to turn her down again, when she said those words—*those* words. Those words every Jewish man longs to hear, those words that touched me to my very core and changed my mind completely. "Please, Shlomo—money's no object."

I worked for Rivka for the next six months, though perhaps "work" is not the most accurate term. A better description might be, "I floated on air with Rivka for the next six months." I introduced her to every logical candidate I could find—a cantor from Kansas, a lawyer from Louisiana, a mohel from Miami. None were right. And then, a funny thing happened. Rivka and I started getting closer. We've been dating now for a year and a half, and our only argument so far has been which of us is luckier to be with the other. Nauseating, I know. I even gave her a refund on her money—which hurt.

But, Rivka and I both learned that sometimes the thing you want most in life is right in front of you, if you'll only open your eyes. And another thing—real happiness and fulfillment *is* all it's cracked up to be. Why, I'll have days and even weeks in which I don't even think about that money I returned to her. I guess that's love. Or my memory's failing. It's all in a day's work for Shlomo Rabinowitz, Jewish Private Eye and Dating Specialist. L'chaim, y'all.

Dating Boot Camp

A modern-day phenomenon of the exercise movement is the fitness boot camp. It's a kinder, gentler version of the Army basic training boot camp, where you can sign up to get into shape through an intensive, no-nonsense exercise program. These are offered by various organizations throughout Santa Monica. I see them regularly in the park where I jog. They're pretty easy to identify. It's always three or four ripped, chiseled, impossibly fit male and female "drill sergeants," sometimes in camouflage outfits, putting ten dumpy-looking male and female "recruits" through the paces of nonstop exercise routines. This all happens very early in the morning, and the masochists, I mean recruits, actually pay the drill sergeants for this abuse.

This is all well and good for the physical fitness portion of your life, but what about the dating portion? For those of us eager to get our dating lives on the fast track to success, shouldn't there be a dating boot camp? It's only logical. It could work. Hell, we've tried everything else. Perhaps I'll start one myself. Lord knows I have the experience; I've lived through the pain, been through dating hell and back. I can envision myself appearing à la General George S. Patton, giving the opening address to my recruits:

"At ease, singles . . . Humans love to meet the opposite sex. All real humans love the sting and clash of dating. You are here today for one reason—to prepare to meet your soul mate. Humans love couples. Humans will not tolerate a lonely single. Santa Monicans despise lonely singles. I wouldn't give a hoot in hell for a single who didn't try his damndest to become a couple. That's why Santa Monicans have never lost nor will ever lose the desire to hook up. Now I want you to remember that no bastard ever won a date by sitting home alone. He won it by dating so many women that he forced the other poor dumb bastard to sit home alone. God, how I love the smell of dating in the morning!"

A close examination of the fitness boot camp's features reveals aspects that could easily be translated into a dating boot camp. Take the obstacle course. The dating obstacle course could involve jumping over your date's overprotective relatives, scaling the walls of their secure apartment building, lifting the baggage of their previous relationships, climbing greased ropes to prove your level of commitment, and dodging their other current dates who are trying to tackle you and put you out of commission.

In the nutritional counseling section, women would practice ordering small salads for their meals in restaurants to prove that they are weight-conscious and not out to break their dates' wallets. Men would learn to eat with new things called utensils and that a napkin is almost as convenient to use as a sleeve.

The sprints are an important part of the dating fitness program. You'll practice sprinting to get to your coffee date on time—and then sprinting away even faster once you realize that hell freezing over would be the next time you'd want to see him or her again.

Let's not forget body fat testing, which you'll learn how to do visually. You'll become adept at sizing up your prospective partner and answering the eternal question, "In an intimate situation, could this person possibly accidentally crush me to death?" And if you happen to find yourself in that particular position, you'll learn which nerve of theirs to pinch in order to disable them and escape, completely uncrushed and almost as good as new.

A dating boot camp would sculpt, tone, and reduce your excess dating fat and also improve your emotional strength and commitment endurance. You'd develop more dating energy and an overall sense that you deserve to meet your soul mate, are ready to meet your soul mate, and by God, will meet your soul mate. Convinced? Then let's get started with a dating fitness march to Starbucks. "Hup . . . hup . . . hup . . . hup . . . I don't know but I've been told (YOU REPEAT) . . . I will date 'fore I get old (YOU REPEAT) . . . Sound off . . . I can't HEAR you . . . "

Skip Dating—Go Directly to Marriage

Like most everyone, I was brought up to believe that romance and falling in love is indeed a very specific, time-tested process. Everyone seems to think that after you meet someone, you need to date for a while (sometimes for years) and then eventually decide if you want to marry this person. After years in the dating scene, I started to tire of it. In fact, dating felt like a never-ending job interview. And, since as we all know the divorce rate is over 50 percent, any reasonable person might conclude that there has to be a better way of finding romantic happiness.

Unbeknownst to me, at another location in the city, a woman named Kathy had similarly reached the end of her dating rope and was about to purchase sperm from a cryobank. How did I discover that? By striking up a conversation with her later that night at a restaurant as we waited for our to-go pizzas.

Chemistry kicked in, and by the time our pizzas were ready, we decided to share a table and eat right there.

What followed was the traditional Exchanging of the Dating Horror Stories, along with much laughter and mutual attraction. She told me about one date who still lived at home with his parents, had no car or job, and cried during sex.

Whether it was our shared past dating hell, our shared two bottles of wine, or simply that we were two people who'd met at the right time in our lives and couldn't immediately see any drawbacks or red flags—we were bonding rather quickly. I felt it. Kathy felt it.

The next night, we went out on our first date, and dinner went great. We shared our thoughts on marriage and came to the same conclusion: at some point, you just pick someone. And so as I walked Kathy to her car, an incredible thought occurred to me. You decide that he or she is The One. I looked at her and asked myself, what if Kathy is The One? And what if she's thinking that I might be The One? How to tell, how to tell? We were almost at her car.

And then I said: "I realize we don't know each other very well and haven't known each other very long. But we've agreed that at some point you have to just choose someone. And so I choose you." I asked her to marry me. I immediately pointed out that since neither of us has had luck doing things the traditional way . . . who's to say that this crazy idea of getting married this quickly wouldn't be more effective?

Kathy said yes! I asked her if we could get married at the end of the week. She said yes and then I said yes. We agreed that we could make this work. In fact, we were determined to make it work. I made it clear that I was not playing games. Again, she agreed and said neither was she. We both laughed about the fact that we would not have sex until we were married—which would be within the week. Then Kathy realized that she was now actually engaged . . . so she called her best friend. Then I called mine, and naturally both our friends immediately tried to talk us out of getting married. In fact, everyone who heard our plan tried to talk us out of it. But we were impervious to logic.

Everything was happening so fast, and we both got caught up in the excitement. The next few days went by like a movie montage of wonderful dates. Movies, restaurants, walks in the park, museums, walking dogs.

Our families were convinced we were insane, and we didn't disagree with them. Still, we realized that most of our friends who'd dated for years before getting married were no longer together. Kathy and I were just collapsing the time span of two of life's occurrences—courtship and marriage. We celebrated our 24-hour anniversary. We were in love and we were nuts, and that was enough for us.

Most couples spend a year planning their wedding. We thought that was a little long, so we gave ourselves a day. And it went by in a blur. A hotel employee friend got us a banquet room for an hour—squeezed in between two other couples' weddings. Like whirling dervishes, we chose the cake, food, booze, flowers, band, photographer, priest, and rabbi. We composed and sent out the e-mail invitations, followed by invitations to our impromptu bachelor and bachelorette parties. What we lacked in being selective, we more than made up for in speed. We picked every element of our wedding the same way we picked each other—quickly and by our gut feeling.

My bachelor party took place at a club in Greenwich Village. Kathy had hers at a clothing store that was closed for the evening (her friends actually had fun trying on all the outfits that would eventually become their bridesmaid dresses).

At both parties, our best friends continued to warn us about moving too fast and suggested over and over that we reconsider this insanity. Of course neither Kathy nor I would back down . . . because we knew we were in love and that's all that mattered.

At the end of the evening, I met up with Kathy again. We opened up our laptops and checked on our RSVPs for the wedding. We kissed as the sun came up, and it was clear to us that everything was going perfectly . . . so far.

Did things go wrong in all this haste? Sure. The photographer's dog took a big bite out of the cake. The strippers for my bachelor party never showed. But the wedding managed to happen. It took place at the Waldorf Astoria. We watched our one-hour banquet room transformed in the style of a D-day invasion. It was a wedding played out at hyperspeed, and I remember watching everyone as they came roaring in: the band, the caterers, the waiters, the guests, etc. Luckily, I remembered to remind my hotel connection that we would definitely be out of there by 3 PM sharp.

I watched as the room was instantly transformed, seats were taken, and the wedding began. Then Kathy finally made her entrance and, of course, she looked fantastic. Amidst the madness, all I chose to focus on was how beautiful Kathy looked in her dress. And how sincerely we exchanged our vows, which we'd written together in forty-five minutes.

The food was served in seconds and removed in seconds. This was followed by a quick first dance, very short speeches, picture-taking, cake-cutting, etc. It was all exhausting and hilarious insanity.

Both of us had to be back at work Monday morning, so we only had one full day for our honeymoon. Not nearly enough, but we made the most of Cancun anyway. Yes, that's right. We crammed a one-week honeymoon into a one-day honeymoon.

We raced to JFK and managed to catch our plane. Yes, we were both a bit concerned about our separate careers, but then we realized we didn't have to worry so much, as we would be back in the city tomorrow.

When we got to Cancun, we attempted to accomplish in twenty-four hours what most tourists would attempt to accomplish in a month. I do have to admit that Kathy and I had our first fight in the cab, but we had too much to do to have any kind of time-consuming argument. The next morning, when we got back on the plane, Kathy and I were so tired that we weren't really speaking to each other all that much. I think this might have been the first sign that things were starting to go wrong. But by the time we landed, we reassured one another that we were still very much in love and ready to make this work. In the cab ride back to the city, my guess is that we both were starting to recognize the fact that we were about to move in with each other, but really didn't know each other at all. Twenty-four hours later, we were back in the city and Kathy moved into my apartment.

Once we agreed that Kathy would move into my apartment, we discovered that our lifestyles were quite distinct. When we woke up that morning, we continued to notice that we didn't exactly have everything in common. I had been up since 6 AM and was busy exercising. Kathy was obviously a very slow riser. While I drank my protein shake, Kathy lit up a cigarette.

And as time went on, Kathy and I discovered that we were more different than alike. We had little arguments that escalated into bigger ones. After three days as man and wife, we visited a marriage counselor. The counselor said what we'd both been thinking. What did we really expect after marrying each other and only knowing one another for less than a week?

And so we agreed on a trial separation. Of course, we still had to meet with lawyers and file for an annulment . . . but after we left the lawyer's office, we walked through the park and had the greatest conversation we've ever had. I have to admit it was more like a traditional first date, and we began to truly get to know each other. I asked her what her favorite movie was and she asked me to explain what I really did for a living. By the time we exited the park, we both realized we wanted to go out on a date Saturday night.

Both of us have had to reluctantly admit that no matter how repetitive and boring dating can be, it's just one of those things we all have to do. Getting to really know someone does take time, so dating is just a necessary evil that we're all going to have to endure as we continue the search for our soul mate.

SECTION FOUR:
FUN "NEWS" STORIES I WROTE ABOUT ROMANCE, DATING, AND THE SEXES

The following is a strictly fun section. Of course, you'll be the judge of that. Here are a number of fake news stories I wrote for a national humor tabloid called *Weekly World News*,[1] similar to *The Onion*. The challenge was to write "news" stories that appeared to be actual true news stories, even though they were not. I've chosen ones here that deal with dating, the sexes, sex, and relationships. In food terms, think of these as the sorbet following the book's main courses. Or, if you prefer a more substantial dessert—chocolate cake or pecan pie. For you healthy folks—fresh fruit. Now, what other book entertains you and feeds you according to your dietary preferences? And you don't even have to dress up or leave your house.

Female God Recalls Man for Repairs

Vatican City—In a sign that God may be taking an increasingly more personal interest in human affairs, a man has been recalled to Heaven for the first time—for repairs—by God, who has revealed Herself as female. According to Vatican spokesperson Claude Duteil, God's Human Recall Notice has been received and presented to the man in question. "While we are not at liberty to disclose his name, I can tell you some things about him, which will explain why he was recalled," reveals Duteil.

"The man is a shameless womanizer who devotes the majority of his time and energy to indulging in pleasures of the flesh, of the bottle, and of material possessions." Apparently, not only does the man have absolutely no regrets about his behavior, but he even teaches a seminar enlightening other men about his techniques. God, the forgiving spirit that She is, decided it was time to give the man a spiritual makeover.

"He will be in Heaven for approximately six weeks," states Duteil, "staying at the newly created Divine Human Makeover Facility, where teams of angel technicians will reprogram his internal priorities, ethics, and spirituality circuits—and then return him to Earth, where, although he will look the same, you will find a remarkably different man." Other parts of the Divine Human Makeover Facility include a Sensitivity Training workshop, a Women Are People, Too seminar, an Alcohol Hypnosis technique, which will actually cause the man to become violently nauseated at the very thought of booze, and a Less Is More intensive, which will cause the man to truly believe that he can be happier with fewer material possessions.

The revelation that God is a female is causing major shockwaves throughout the religious world. One church is placing pink velvet book covers on all its Bibles. The world's finest counterfeit portrait artists are repainting religious masterpiece paintings so that they portray God as a woman. A major recruiting effort is underway to have more women trained as priests, rabbis, and spiritual leaders of all denominations. And the Vatican has offered a guarantee that its next pope will definitely be a woman. "We were planning on having a woman pope, anyway," reveals Duteil.

The human recall is also affecting behavior throughout the world, with crime rates having dropped 37 percent since God's Human Recall Notice arrived. "I've never seen the city so quiet and crime-free," says New York City Police Captain Lawrence Tibble. "Citizens are polite, considerate, on their best behavior—it's really eerie." One citizen, Vinnie Testosterini, explains, "Of course we're on our best behavior. Nobody wants to be recalled and have to go through all that reprogramming. Besides, you never know when God, being a woman, could get all emotional on ya and send ya to that other place. No offense, God."

5 Biggest Secrets Women Don't Want Men to Know

Bethesda, Maryland—Women, often considered "the mysterious sex," will now be a bit less mysterious, thanks to the recently leaked document, "5 Biggest Secrets About Women They Don't Want Men to Know!" The eye-opening document was leaked by an insider at the all-female National Women's Research Institute in Bethesda, Maryland. "When we find out which of our employees leaked those survey results," states NWRI spokeswoman Melanie Aroyan, "she'll be fired—and sued. And if it was up to me, she'd also be horsewhipped."

The document consists of the survey answers of more than 10,000 women of all ages and ethnic groups to the question, "As a woman, what is it about you that you would never want men to know?" The survey results were never meant to be revealed to men, as they represent the deepest secrets women have about their gender.

Here, from the survey's summation page, are the 5 Biggest Secrets About Women They Don't Want Men to Know:

1. **Women's Public Bathrooms Are Lush Havens Beyond Men's Wildest Dreams.** If a man mistakenly enters a woman's public bathroom, he'll see what appears to be an ordinary restroom. Only women, however, know the location of the secret sliding panel in each women's restroom that opens to reveal the hidden, deluxe section. This section features wild, tropical plants; hunky, naked male models offering sensual massages; the live music of a classical quartet; a Jacuzzi and sauna; luscious gourmet foods and wines; attendants offering manicures, pedicures, and bikini waxes; an upscale clothing boutique; and current movies on large-screen TVs.

2. **Women Are Just Pretending to Have Periods.** There's no such thing as menstrual cycles and periods. It's something women simply made up to give themselves a one-week reprieve from men's nonstop groping and pawing in bed. And, yes, the tampon companies are all run by women and are in on the scam. Women get a refund check from the tampon companies at the end of each year for a percentage of their tampon purchases.

3. **Women Crave Sex Even More Than Men Do.** If men knew that, though, it would throw off the whole balance of sexual power that is now clearly in women's favor. For this reason, women must maintain the illusion that what's between their legs is gold and to be rationed judiciously.

4. **Every Woman is Bisexual.** Women just pretend to be upset when a relationship with a man comes to an end.

In reality, that's their perfect opportunity to immediately begin or resume a passionate relationship with one of their many hot female friends.

5. **Women Will Take Over the Planet in the Year 2025.** Since it has already been proven that women are smarter, more resourceful, emotionally stronger, more attractive, and live longer than men, it only makes sense that they, and not men, should run the world. They have been planning to take over the planet for the past 150 years. They hope to do so in a nonviolent fashion, but are nonetheless prepared to do so by any means necessary.

Amish Phone Sex Chat Line a Huge Hit

The world's first Amish phone sex chat line has become so popular that it is attracting one thousand new Amish callers daily! AmishPhoneChatCo President Jebediah Stoltzfus, of Lancaster, Pennsylvania, saw a need and filled it. "Young Amish men and women have a great curiosity about life and about one another. I'm just providing a means for them to communicate. Plus, the first hundred callers each day get a free quart of Pennsylvania Dutch German potato salad."

Stoltzfus provided the following partial transcript of a typical AmishPhoneChat call:

REBECCA: I am Rebecca. And who might thee be?

SAMUEL: I am Samuel. And I am dripping with sweat from the barn raising.

REBECCA: I, too, am moist, Samuel—from the day's plowing.

SAMUEL: Perhaps we shall plow together one day, God willing.

REBECCA: I'd like that. And then we can churn butter.

SAMUEL: Thou art exciting me. What art thou wearing?

REBECCA: I am attired in my shapeless, floor-length black dress with a black bonnet and sensible shoes, but I have just undone the top button of the thirty-seven buttons on my plain, formless blouse.

SAMUEL: If our religion did not forbid the use of electricity, I would ask thee to a movie.

REBECCA: Forgive me, Samuel—I keep thinking of how you'd look without your big black hat on.

Encouraged by the success of his Amish phone sex chat line, Stoltzfus is proceeding with plans for marketing the first Amish automobile. "We are forbidden to drive an actual motorized car, so it will be the body of a Chevy made to fit perfectly over a horse."

10 Best Opening Lines to Get Republican Women into Bed

The results of an exciting new survey reveal the ten best opening lines most effective in convincing a Republican woman to offer a man a night of bed-pounding, back-scratching, hot monkey love! The survey appears in *Political Psychology Today* magazine and was led by Dr. Jedediah Leland of the Institute for Socio-Sexual Research. "In addition to the opening lines, we discovered a number of truly surprising insights," reveals Dr. Leland. "First, three times as many Democrat men as Republican men want to have sex with Republican women. When we asked them why, the Democrat men responded that they had a strong urge to do to these women what the Republican party has done to the country."

Also, Republican women turned out to be moaners, as opposed to Democrat women, who were primarily screamers. Dr. Leland's theory: "Democrat women are still so upset about their party's political losses that sex just makes them vocalize this disappointment all the more."

Dr. Leland further adds that 87 percent of Republican women, while providing oral sex to men, hum "Hail to the Chief." He states, "We have no explanation for this, but none of the men complained. In fact, many told us it's now their favorite song."

Here are the survey's 10 Best Opening Lines to Get Republican Women Into Bed:

1. You know, in this light, when you smile that certain way, you look like you could be Sarah Palin's younger, more desirable sister.
2. Sorry if I seem aggravated—I'm still upset about that world-class jerk, Michael Moore.
3. Allow me to buy you a drink. After all, thanks to the new Republican Congress, the economy has never been better!
4. I'd love to hang out with you, but I can't make it a late night—I'm shipping out to Fallujah in the morning.
5. The tattoo on my penis spells "RAN." But when I get excited, it spells "REPUBLICAN."
6. If I had to choose between having a Republican president in the White House for the rest of this century or never being able to see your cleavage again, I'd be stumped.
7. I'm all for No Child Left Behind. I'm even more for *your* child-like behind.
8. To see you naked, I would turn in my own mother to the Department of Homeland Security.
9. Just as the Republican Party boldly confronts big challenges, nothing would please me more than your

confronting the big challenge rapidly growing right now in my pants.

10. Because of the Republican Congress's leadership, we are strong; because of its vision, we will be even stronger; and because I can't stop thinking about the magic between your legs, I haven't been able to stand up for the last half hour.

Spain Claims It Originated French Kissing—and Sues France for $6 Billion!

Madrid, Spain—Ever heard of "Spanish kissing"? You will if the Spanish government wins its current lawsuit against France. Spain is claiming that the world's most passionate and popular kiss—the open-mouthed French kiss—originated, not in France, but in Spain in 1605! "And we have documentation to back that up," states Julio Salazar, president of the Society for the Promotion of Spanish Kissing, which is spearheading the lawsuit.

Salazar refers to what is perhaps Spain's most famous novel, *Don Quixote of la Mancha*, by Miguel de Cervantes. In the following passage from the novel, published in 1605, Cervantes describes how the buxom country girl, Dulcinea, kisses a peasant man: "Dulcinea and Pedro kissed with all their heart and with their mouths fully open, tongues exploring tongues, teeth, lips, mouth. Poor Sancho got overheated watching them. But

Dulcinea explained that it was the only way lovers kissed in her village and in the surrounding villages as well."

Salazar accuses France of stealing the Spanish kiss, claiming it as its own, and promoting it throughout the world as the French kiss. "For centuries, romantic couples have been flocking to Paris as the city of love, partially due to the image of the 'French kiss,'" explains Salazar. That cost Spain an untold fortune in tourist dollars. It's time to recover some of those dollars—and return the Spanish kiss to its rightful originator!"

Relatives Commit Woman for Dating Old Flame— an Actual Old Flame!

Hephzibah, Georgia—Renee Corben hadn't gone out with a man for over three years—ever since her boyfriend Carl left her for another woman. "I've had the worst luck with men," revealed Corben. "I've dated guys I later came to find out couldn't commit, were drug and alcohol abusers, lazy, promiscuous, abusive, and reckless." So when Corben told her friends and family she was dating an old flame, they were just happy she was back in the dating saddle. Their happiness faded, however, when they discovered that the old flame Corben was dating was an actual old flame, from a candle! "I'm worried about her," admitted Corben's aunt, Patrice, who spearheaded the Corben family movement to have Corben taken in for psychological evaluation. "Renee has obviously gone off the deep end."

But her fling with the flame makes perfect sense to Corben, who was interviewed inside her padded room at the Hephzibah

Mental Health Facility. "Look, men have been one disappointment after another. So I finally just sat down one night, poured myself a glass of wine, lit a candle, and made a list of the things I wanted from a romantic relationship. Turns out I wanted someone who was warm, who'd light up my life, who'd always be there for me, and who could spend hours in the same room with me without talking and still feel comfortable. None of the men I'd met had those qualities.

"But suddenly, as I was gazing into the candlelight, it occurred to me that the candle had all of those qualities. It had been right in front of my nose all these years, and I never noticed. So I decided then and there that if the candle was giving me everything I desired from a romantic relationship, I might as well start dating the candle. And so I did. I take it to movies and restaurants; I've introduced it to all my friends and family. And when it burns down, I just replace it with a brand-new one. I realize this is a bit unusual, but I swear to you that I've never been happier—or more in love! Alan, which is what I've named him, is truly my hunk of burning love!"

Police Arrest Woman Who Claims She Simply Loved Her Boyfriend to Pieces!

Wetumpka, Alabama—When Andy Fleder's parents didn't hear from their son for several days, they suspected something was very wrong. "Andy always returned our phone calls," said his tearful mother Maggie. "We couldn't even get hold of his girlfriend, Darlene. That's when we decided to contact the police."

Wetumpka police found no trace of Fleder at his apartment, work, or friends' homes, and launched an extensive search. "We finally found him just outside Wetumpka, in a Burger Deli dumpster," revealed police sergeant Jeremy Kellerman. "Unfortunately, the bloodhounds also found parts of him in an alley beside a movie theater in Clanton, in a park in Opelika, beside a flower shop in Tuscumbia, and at a lovers' lane in Gadsden."

But this was no ordinary homicide. The mystery was solved during intense interrogation of Darlene. "She told us she loved

Andy to pieces," recalled Kellerman. "I told her that's just an expression, but she said, 'You're wrong. My love for Andy was so intense that I hugged him with every part of my body, with all my might. The next thing I knew—the man I loved just broke! He fell apart.'"

Darlene explained she buried the body not to conceal it, but to put him to rest in places that meant something to both of them during their two-year relationship. Oddly, Darlene is happy to be in police custody. "Without the light of my life, I have nowhere else to go. Besides, it's dangerous for me to be on my own. The other day my drapes caught fire. You see, I still carry a torch for Andy."

Couple Spontaneously Combust While Having Sex!

Many people look forward to the prospect of hot sex, but one couple's lovemaking got so steamy, they suddenly burst into flames and vanished into thin air! Jenna Hambrick, 23, and Randy Foyer, 27, of Queensland, Australia, had an extremely active love life, according to their next-door neighbor, Pete McGuinn. "Oh, yes. They went at each other like wild beasts, at all hours of the day and night. They had no pets, but you would think there was a zoo in there with all the hootin' and hollerin' they did. I mean, here we are, me and the missus, trying to have a quiet Sunday tea, and for hours it's 'Oh, God, don't stop!' and 'Jungle Beast, I want you now!' and 'I need you inside me!' We felt lucky our children were grown and out of the house!"

On the night in question, Jenna and Randy had invited home with them a young woman, Eliza Perkins, 21, whom they had met that evening at a local bar. After a few hours of sex between the three of them, Eliza excused herself to use the bathroom. She remembers the scene vividly when she returned: "Jenna and Randy was, y'know, really gettin' into it, sweatin' like a couple of demons, screamin' with pleasure, the bed rocking. And just as they're both reachin', um, the big O, there was a small explosion as they both burst into flames and disappeared. I mean there was nothing left—no bodies, no ashes—it was like they was never there."

Sergeant Garth Enoch of the Queensland Royal Police was not surprised. "Oh, yeah, we get two or three 'Flamers,' as we call 'em, every month. Kind of sad, really, especially for the relatives. Though you do save some money on the casket. And, of course, also on the positive side, that's probably one of your better ways to go, if you have to go. I mean, that's how I'd want to exit planet Earth. Not that I'm planning on it. It's just thoughts."

Scientists have studied the phenomenon of spontaneous combustion for years, according to Professor Hugh Belkin, Chairman of the Biology Department at the University of Southern Queensland. "Over the past 300 years, there have been more than 200 reports of persons burning to a crisp for no apparent reason—though in many of the cases, extreme sexual relations seems to be a contributing factor. The fascinating part of it for me is that the fire is both so incredibly intense and comes from within the human body."

Oddly enough, for all the years it's been studied, no satisfactory explanation of spontaneous human combustion has ever been given. It is still an unsolved mystery. But it is not by any means the only mysterious way people have died. According to Professor Belkin, other documented strange

Men's Least Effective Pickup Lines

There are scores of books, websites, and seminars out there informing men about the most effective opening lines to use to meet women. Now, at long last, a major survey reveals the *least* effective pickup lines! "Use any of these lines to try to meet a woman, and you're guaranteed to receive either a slap in the face, a kick in the groin, or a restraining order," claims Charles Gayton, director of Survey America, Inc., the company that just completed the five-year, 2,500-women survey. "They will invariably leave the woman either repulsed, deeply offended, nauseated, or, most likely, a combination of all three."

The women surveyed were simply asked one question: "What was the least effective, most offensive opening line you've ever heard from a man trying to meet you?" There were no shortage of answers, according to Gayton. "Most women had at least ten that still bothered them, even after several years." But several of the opening lines were used over and over again by many of the men—and created the maximum disgust level.

Here, according to the survey, are the world's least effective pickup lines:

PATRIOTIC:

- "I'm shipping out to Afghanistan in the morning. Want to come back to my place and help me grease my rifle?"
- "God bless the flag, God bless America, and God bless the person who created that Wonderbra you're wearing!"
- "Do you like patriotic songs? Come out to my car with me and I'll sing you my favorite. It's called 'Yank My Doodle, It's a Dandy.'"

BOASTING:

- "Would you like to meet God? I can set it up. He's a good friend."
- "You ever been to Stockholm? I'm looking for a date to come with me when I pick up my Nobel Prize for Passion."
- "Can you recommend a good plastic surgeon specializing in penis reduction?"

TRICKERY:

- "OK, when I snap my fingers, you will awaken, fully refreshed, have no memory of being hypnotized, and will try to impress me with your being an insatiable nymphomaniac."
- "Let's flip a coin. Heads—you come home and sleep with me. Tails—I come home and sleep with you."
- "I'll be honest. I'm a frog, and only a kiss from you

can remove the curse and turn me into a prince. Let me just explain exactly where on me you need to kiss for it to be effective."

YUCK!:

- "I've shaved my back hair to reveal the words 'I Love You.'"
- "Allow me to buy you a drink—my living at home with my parents allows me a monthly chunk of boozing income."
- "Hey, babe, in case your biological clock is ticking, I'm ready, willing, and able to do my part tonight."

Woman Divorces Man After Discovering the "Mint" He Made Was Just Candy!

Blue Ridge, Georgia—Unlike many career-oriented women today, Bonnie Kegel never particularly desired a college education, a fulfilling career, or having the ability to support herself. As did several generations of her family's women, Kegel had just one objective in her life. And as traditional and outdated as it was, nonetheless Kegel wanted it with all her heart and soul: to find a wealthy man to support her in style.

"So, naturally I was very excited to meet Edward Pellingham at a dance," explained Kegel. "His name even sounds rich, doesn't it? Edward Pellingham. He was charming, crazy about me, and confided to me that he made a real mint last year and fully expected to make another mint this year, next year, and every year for the foreseeable future. I started feeling faint. This was my dream come true!"

Pellingham asked Kegel to marry him immediately, and she agreed. "I considered my future with Edward, and it looked bright. I had visions of exquisite jewelry, luxury vacations, thrilling homes, cars, and boats." The magic didn't last long. After one day of marriage, Kegel filed for divorce. "Though I'd prefer an annulment—to make it like the marriage never happened. That man clearly mislead me."

Pellingham never really made a mint? "Oh, he made a mint all right," revealed Kegel. "A candy mint, as it turns out! Can you believe the nerve of that guy, getting me all excited about being with a man who makes a mint every year? The guy turns out to be unemployed, living in a mobile home, and spends his days watching TV, making mint candies, and misleading women like me. They oughta lock him away!" Still trying to win her back, Pellingham offered to treat her to pearls. "But I'm not falling for that one," stated Kegel. "I happen to have noticed there's a greasy spoon diner near his mobile home called Pearl's Home Cooking."

EPILOGUE

An Apology to Female Daters (Especially the Ones I've Dated)

Hello, ladies. First, the gratitude: Thank you for reading my book. Thank you for being the smarter sex. Thank you for being the more attractive sex. And, of course, thank you for the sex. Without you, the world would be colder, less colorful, less intelligent, less caring, and less fun. Plus, the whole birth thing would be far more challenging. Without you, this book would not exist; nor would I. You are life. You are love. And, if I may be so bold, you are more delicious than chocolate.

Now, the apology part. Look, we male daters can let on that we're all that, that we've got it going on, we're hip, sexy, accomplished, manly, strong, creative, God's gift to women and to the planet. We can showcase our laurels 'til the cows come home—which is a long time, especially if you live in a city.

But the fact is—we men are flawed. Sorry, didn't mean to shock you. It's just that for all the plusses we have, we have at least an equal number of problems, drawbacks, and disadvantages. If we were a product, we should be returned to the store immediately for a refund or store credit. Oh, all right, I'll speak for myself. I'm flawed. Despite my letting on like I'm some sort of dating guru, the fact of the matter is, though I've done some things right, I've also done women wrong, behaved in ways of which I'm not proud, made countless mistakes. And so I'd like to come clean and ask your forgiveness.

Consider it my dating penance. So, have a seat, pour yourself a drink, and . . .

Please consider forgiving me for, from time to time, over the years:

- Leaving a good relationship too soon
- Staying too long in a bad relationship
- Being impatient
- Being judgmental
- Being unappreciative
- Being unhelpful
- Not being understanding
- Being insensitive
- Taking too little care with my appearance
- Failing to nurture the relationship
- Failing to put things into perspective
- Not taking responsibility for things that are clearly my fault
- Writing about life and love rather than living it
- Not sharing my innermost feelings
- The Superman tattoo in that very special place

Well, I could go on, but the publisher gave me a page limit. You get the idea. Plenty of room for improvement. We're all works in progress, aren't we? There's no one correct way to do love, dating, and relationships. No government-endorsed manual. It's not taught in school. Granted, there are so-called dating gurus and relationship experts, but all they're giving is their informed opinions. Each person is different and each relationship is different.

Ultimately, it comes down to us feeling around in the relationship dark (which, by the way, is not a bad dating activity), trusting our gut feelings, trying to do unto others romantically the way we'd like others to do unto us. That's my all-important Golden Dating Rule. And it only took me 500 dates to discover it! Thank you for understanding and forgiving. If you ever need something similar, I'm here for you.

Your apologetic friend and fellow survivor of the online dating wars,

Mark

A Word of Gratitude, Encouragement, and Hope to My Fellow Male Daters

Dear Fellow Male Daters:

Thank you so much for spending time with my book. It's my first one, so it means a lot to me. Remember how much your first girl meant to you? Take a few moments now to indulge in those sweet memories . . . OK, enough. You had to take it that far, didn't you?

I know you have many other literary choices and the fact that you chose mine over those of Shakespeare, Hemingway, or Aristotle—the authors to whom I am most often compared—is so flattering. And a special thanks to those of you who actually paid for this book. You know who you are. And I so respect and admire you.

But whether you're a male dater who parted with your hard-earned cash to acquire this book or one of the slackers who got it from the library or found it on the lawn at a yard sale, in between the wooden salad bowls and the VHS copy of *Bill and Ted's Excellent Adventure,* I feel your pain. Whatever your dating complaints, challenges, disappointments, failures, and nightmares are, all I can say is, "I know, I know." I've covered many of mine in this book, so hopefully you don't feel so alone, or at least any more alone than you usually feel on a Saturday night when it's just you, HBO and a pint of Häagen-Dazs. Yes, I know all about that, too. From the drone satellite, of course. And quit leaving your clothing on the floor. But I digress.

I also know about your dating joys, pleasures, successes, little victories, passions, and assorted delights. Because many of you bombard the world with them on Facebook. As do I with mine. Hopefully, I've shared some of those plusses herein as well. The point is, as with most things in life, dating offers the good and the bad, the positive and the negative, the yin and the yang, the fire and the rain. And while whining and complaining about the negative aspects is a healthy way to air and purge those frustrations, the fully evolved dater realizes they're simply a part of the overall dating pie. One day, I hope to become exactly such a fully evolved human being, one who can communicate without resorting to sugar-laden dessert metaphors.

If I can leave you with any final thought, it's this: For a healthy morning breakfast, nothing beats a fresh fruit smoothie. But back on topic—however long, involved, rocky, and painful the journey we need to undertake en route to our relationship nirvana, it's worth it. I don't need to prove that to you because if you've ever had a soul mate, a wonderful romantic relationship, or even witnessed one in a Scarlett Johansson movie, then you know.

I would, therefore, simply encourage you to proceed on your romantic journey with a loving heart, an open mind, the patience of a saint, and a firm resolve to keep the hair on the back of your neck groomed. A fuzzy neck can be a real romantic buzz kill. Or, uh, so I've heard.

Other than that, I just wanted to wish you luck because, truly, it comes down to that so often. I genuinely hope that you find the woman of your dreams. And if my humble little book has played even a small part in making that happen, well, then, you owe me big-time. A gift certificate to Bed Bath & Beyond would be perfect. But, no pressure. Surprise me.

Your friend and fellow survivor of the online dating wars,

Mark

HOW TO KEEP IN TOUCH WITH ME
Follow me on my website/blog
http://www.markmillerhumorist.com/

Follow me on *The Huffington Post*
http://www.huffingtonpost.com/mark-c-miller

Follow me on Facebook
http://www.facebook.com/markmillerhumorist

Follow me on Twitter
http://twitter.com/MarkMiller123

Email
mark@markmillerhumorist.com